Language Change

Jean Aitchison has been lecturer in linguistics at the London School of Economics since 1965. Her interest in language change stems from her study of Greek and Latin at Girton College, Cambridge, England, where she gained a first in classics before going on to study linguistics at Radcliffe College, Cambridge, Massachusetts. She has lectured in several European countries as well as in the USA and has published papers and reviews both on language change and on psycholinguistics. She is the author of *The Articulate Mammal* (Universe, 1983).

Jean Aitchison

Language Change: Progress or Decay?

UNIVERSE BOOKS
New York

To those of my friends,
and particularly Tony,
who think that language change
should be stopped

Published in the United States of America in 1985
by Universe Books
381 Park Avenue South, New York, NY 10016

85 86 87 88 89 / 10 9 8 7 6 5 4 3 2 1

Printed in the United States of America

Library of Congress Cataloging in Publication Data

Aitchison, Jean, 1938-
    Language change.

    Bibliography: p.
    Includes index.
    1. Linguistic change. II. Title.
P142.A37   1985   410   84-24092
ISBN 0-87663-456-0
ISBN 0-87663-872-8 (pbk.)

Contents

Part 4 Beginnings and Endings

Introduction to
Universe Linguistics

In the past twenty-five years, linguistics—the systematic study of language—has come of age. It is a fast expanding and increasingly popular subject, which is now offered as a degree course at a number of universities. As a result of this expansion, psychologists, sociologists, philosophers, anthropologists, teachers, speech therapists and numerous others have realized that language is of crucial importance in their life and work. But when they tried to find out more about the subject, a major problem faced them—the technical and often narrow nature of much writing about linguistics.

The Universe Introductions to Linguistics series is an attempt to solve this problem by presenting current findings in a lucid and non-technical way. Its object is twofold. First, it hopes to outline the 'state of play' in certain crucial areas of the subject, concentrating on what is happening now, rather than on surveying the past. Secondly, it aims to show how linguistics links up with other disciplines such as sociology, psychology, philosophy, speech therapy and language teaching.

The series will, we hope, give readers a fuller understanding of the relationship between language and other aspects of human behavior, as well as equipping those who wish to find out more about the subject with a basis from which to read some of the more technical literature in textbooks and journals.

Jean Aitchison
London School of Economics

Preface

The study of language change – sometimes known as historical linguistics – has altered its character considerably in recent years. Traditionally, scholars concerned themselves with describing sound changes as they unrolled through the ages. In this, they paid relatively little attention to changes currently taking place, or to the sociolinguistic and psycholinguistic factors which underlie many alterations. This book shows how work on changes in progress has widened our knowledge of the nature of language change, as well as indicating the essential importance to historical linguistics of topics once associated more closely with sociology and psychology.

Language change is a topic which, perhaps more than any other, spreads itself over the whole range of areas covered by linguistics. For this reason, the literature often seems disjointed and contradictory, since many scholars, like Jane Austen, prefer to polish their own square inch of ivory, rather than tackle the whole vast subject. Theoretical studies of change, for example, often do not take into account important work being done on changes currently underway, and vice-versa. This book is an attempt to pull all the various strands together into a coherent whole, and to provide an overview of the field as it stands at the moment.

I would like to thank all those colleagues, students and friends who both in discussions and by their writing have helped me to clarify my thoughts on language change. I would also like to mention those teachers from my past who fired my enthusiasm for the subject when I was a student, in particular Professor W. S. Allen and Dr John

Chadwick of Cambridge University, and Professor Roman Jakobson of Harvard University. Finally, I am extremely grateful to those colleagues and friends who have made helpful and often detailed suggestions and comments on this book, in particular (in alphabetical order) Michael Banks (London School of Economics), Raymond Chapman (London School of Economics), Jenny Cheshire (University of Bath), Roger Lass (University of Edinburgh), Melinda Lee, who also did a large amount of the typing (London School of Economics), Peter Mühlhäusler (Oxford University), John Wells (University College, London). I have not always followed their suggestions, so I alone am responsible for any oversimplifications or inaccuracies which may remain.

Most symbols and terms have been explained in the text as they occur, but since several common ones occur more than once, a brief glossary has been added at the end for those readers not familiar with linguistics. Finally, in order to help conquer the all-pervading sexism which exists in the English language, I have sometimes used *she* instead of the conventional *he* in places where a neutral between sexes pronoun is required.

Jean Aitchison

PART 1

Preliminaries

1 *The Ever-whirling Wheel*

The inevitability of change

> Since 'tis Nature's Law to change,
> Constancy alone is strange.
> John Wilmot, Earl of Rochester,
> *A Dialogue between Strephon and Daphne*

Everything in this universe is perpetually in a state of change, a fact commented on by philosophers and poets through the ages. If we flick through any book of quotations we find numerous statements about the fluctuating world we live in: 'Everything rolls on, nothing stays still', claimed the ancient Greek philosopher Heraclitus in the sixth century BC. In the sixteenth century, Edmund Spenser speaks of 'the ever-whirling wheel of change, the which all mortal things doth sway', while 'time and the world are ever in flight' is a statement by the twentieth-century Irish poet William Butler Yeats – to take just a few random examples.

Language, like everything else, joins in this general flux. As the German philosopher-linguist Wilhelm von Humboldt noted in 1836: 'There can never be a moment of true standstill in language, just as little as in the ceaselessly flaming thought of men. By nature it is a continuous process of development. . . .'[1]

Even the simplest and most colloquial English of several hundred years ago sounds remarkably strange to us. Take the work of Robert Mannyng, who wrote a history of England in the mid-fourteenth century. He claimed that he made his language as simple as he could so that ordinary men could understand it, yet it is barely comprehensible to the average person today:

> In symple speche as I couthe,
> That is lightest in mannes mouthe.
> I mad noght for no disours,
> Ne for no seggers, no harpours,
> Bot for the luf of symple men
> That strange Inglis can not ken.[2]

A glance at any page of Chaucer shows clearly the massive changes which have taken place in the last millennium. It is amusing to note that he himself, in *Troylus and Criseyde*, expressed his wonderment that men of long ago spoke in so different a manner from his contemporaries:

> Ye knowe ek, that in forme of speche is chaunge
> Withinne a thousand yer, and wordes tho
> That hadden prys now wonder nyce and straunge
> Us thenketh hem, and yet they spake hem so,
> And spedde as wel in love as men now do.[3]

Language, then, like everything else, gradually transforms itself over the centuries. There is nothing surprising in this. In a world where humans grow old, tadpoles change into frogs, and milk turns into cheese, it would be strange if language alone remained unaltered. As the famous Swiss linguist Ferdinand de Saussure noted: 'Time changes all things: there is no reason why language should escape this universal law.'[4]

In spite of this, large numbers of intelligent people condemn and resent language change, regarding alterations as due to unnecessary sloppiness, laziness or ignorance. Letters are written to newspapers and indignant articles are published, all deploring the fact that new words and new pronunciations are continually coming into existence. The following is a representative sample taken from the last twenty years. In 1968 we find a columnist in a British newspaper complaining about the 'growing unintelligibility of spoken English', and maintaining that 'English used to be a language which foreigners couldn't pronounce but could often understand. Today it is rapidly becoming a language which the English can't pronounce and few foreigners can understand.'[5] At around the same time, another commentator declared angrily that 'through sheer laziness and sloppiness of mind, we are in danger of losing our past subjunctive.'[6] A third owned to 'a queasy distaste for the vulgarity of "between you and I", "these sort", "the media is " . . . precisely the kind of distaste I feel at seeing a damp spoon dipped in the sugar bowl or butter spread with the bread-knife.'[7] In 1972 the writer of an article emotively entitled 'Polluting our language' condemned the 'blind surrender to the momentum or inertia of slovenly and tasteless ignorance and insensitivity'.[8] A reviewer discussing the 1978 edition of the *Pocket Oxford Dictionary* announced that his 'only sadness is that the current editor seems prepared to bow to every slaphappy and slipshod change of meaning'.[9] The author of a book published in 1979 compared a word which changes its meaning to 'a piece of wreckage with a ship's name on it floating away from a sunken hulk': the book was entitled *Decadence*.[10] And in 1980, the literary editor of *The Times* complained that the grammar of English 'is becoming simpler and coarser'.[11]

We can neatly summarize the above views by quoting Ogden Nash's poem, 'Laments for a Dying Language' (1962):

> Coin brassy words at will, debase the coinage;
> We're in an if-you-cannot-lick-them-join age,
> A slovenliness provides its own excuse age,
> Where usage overnight condones misusage.
> Farewell, farewell to my beloved language,
> Once English, now a vile orangutanguage.

The question which immediately springs to mind is the following. Are these objectors merely ludicrous, akin to fools who think it might be possible to halt the movement of the waves or the course of the sun? Are their efforts to hold back the sea of change completely misguided? Alternatively, could these intelligent and, in some cases, well-known men of letters possibly be right? Is it indeed possible that language change is largely due to lack of care and maintenance on our part? Are we simply behaving like the inhabitants of underdeveloped countries who allow tractors and cars to rot after only months of use because they do not understand the need to oil and check the parts every so often? Is it true that 'we need not simply accept it, as though it were some catastrophe of nature. We all talk and we all listen. Each one of us, therefore, every day can break a lance on behalf of our embattled English tongue, by taking a little more trouble', as a *Daily Telegraph* writer claimed?[12] Or, in a slightly modified form, we might ask the following. Even if eventual change is inevitable, can we appreciably retard it, and would it be to our advantage to do so? Furthermore, is it possible to distinguish between 'good' and 'bad' changes, and root out the latter?

These questions often arouse surprisingly strong feelings, and they are not easy to answer. In order to answer them satisfactorily, we need to know considerably more about language change, how it happens, when it happens, who initiates it, and other possible reasons for its occurrence. These are the topics examined in this book. In short, we shall be looking at how and why language change occurs, with the ultimate aim of finding out the direction, if any, in which human languages are moving.

In theory, there are three possibilities to be considered. They could apply either to human language as a whole, or to any one language in particular. The first possibility is slow decay, as was frequently suggested in the last century. Many scholars were convinced that European languages were on the decline because they were gradually losing their old word-endings. For example, the popular

German writer Max Müller asserted that, 'The history of all the Aryan languages is nothing but a gradual process of decay.'[13]

Alternatively, languages might be slowly evolving to a more efficient state. We might be witnessing the survival of the fittest, with existing languages adapting to the needs of the times. The lack of a complicated word-ending system in English might be a sign of streamlining and sophistication, as argued by the Danish linguist Otto Jespersen in 1922: 'In the evolution of languages the discarding of old flexions goes hand in hand with the development of simpler and more regular expedients that are rather less liable than the old ones to produce misunderstandings.'[14]

A third possibility is that language remains in a substantially similar state from the point of view of progress or decay. It may be marking time, or treading water, as it were, with its advance or decline held in check by opposing forces. This is the view of the Belgian linguist Joseph Vendryès, who claimed that 'Progress in the absolute sense is impossible, just as it is in morality or politics. It is simply that different states exist, succeeding each other, each dominated by certain general laws imposed by the equilibrium of the forces with which they are confronted. So it is with language.'[15]

In the course of this book, we shall try to find out where the truth of the matter lies.

The search for purity

Before we look at language change itself, it may be useful to consider why people currently so often disapprove of alterations. On examination, much of it turns out to be based on nothing more than social class prejudice which needs to be stripped away.

Let us begin by asking why the conviction that our language is decaying is so much more widespread than the belief that it is progressing. In an intellectual climate where the notion of the survival of the fittest is at least as strong as the belief in inevitable decay, it is strange that so many people are convinced of the decline in quality of English, a language which is now spoken by an estimated half billion people – a possible hundredfold increase in the number of speakers during the past millennium.

Our first reaction is to wonder whether the members of the anti-slovenliness brigade, as we may call them, are subconsciously reacting to the fast-moving world we live in, and consequently resenting change in any area of life. To some extent this is likely to be true. A feeling that 'fings ain't wot they used to be' and an attempt to preserve life unchanged seem to be natural reactions to insecurity, symptoms of growing old. Every generation inevitably believes that the clothes, manners and speech of the following one have deteriorated. We would therefore expect to find a respect for conservative language in every century and every culture and, in literate societies, a reverence for the language of the 'best authors' of the past. We would predict a mild nostalgia, typified perhaps by a native speaker of Kru, one of the Niger-Congo group of languages. When asked if it would be acceptable to place the verb at the end of a particular sentence, instead of in the middle where it was usually placed, he replied that this was the 'real Kru' which his father spoke.[16]

In Europe, however, the feeling that language is on the decline seems more widely spread and stronger than the predictable mood of mild regret. On examination, we find that today's laments take their place in a long tradition of complaints about the corruption of language. Similar expressions of horror were common in the nineteenth century. In 1858 we discover a certain Reverend A. Mursell fulminating against the use of phrases such as *hard up, make oneself scarce, shut up.*[17] At around the same time in Germany, Jacob Grimm, one of the Brothers Grimm of folk tale fame, stated nostalgically that 'six hundred years ago every rustic knew, that is to say practised daily, perfections and niceties in the German language of which the best grammarians nowadays do not even dream.'[18]

Moving back into the eighteenth century, we find the puristic movement at its height. Utterances of dismay and disgust at the state of the language followed one another thick and fast, expressed with far greater urgency than we normally find today. Famous outbursts included that of 1710 when Dean Swift, writing in *The Tatler*, launched an attack on the condition of English. He followed this up two years later with a letter to the Lord Treasurer urging the formation of an academy to regulate language usage, since even the best authors of the age, in his opinion, committed 'many gross improprieties which . . . ought to be discarded'.[19] In 1755, Samuel Johnson's famous dictionary of the English language was published. He stated in the preface that 'Tongues, like governments, have a natural tendency to degeneration,' urging that 'we retard what we cannot repel, that we palliate what we cannot cure.' In 1762, Robert Lowth, Bishop of London, complained that 'the English Language hath been much cultivated during the last 200 years . . . but . . . it hath made no advances in Grammatical accuracy'. He himself attempted to lay down 'rules' of good usage, because 'our best Authors for want of some rudiments of this type have sometimes fallen into mistakes, and been guilty of palpable error in point of Grammar.'[20]

In short, expressions of disgust about language, and proposals for remedying the situation, were at their height in the eighteenth century. Such widespread linguistic fervour has never been paralleled. Let us therefore consider what special factors caused such obsessive worry about language at this time.

Around 1700, English spelling and usage were in a fairly fluid state. Against this background, two powerful social factors combined to convert a normal mild nostalgia for the language of the past into a quasi-religious doctrine. The first was a long-standing admiration for Latin, and the second was powerful class snobbery.

The admiration for Latin was a legacy from its use as the language of the church in the Middle Ages, and as the common language of European scholarship from the Renaissance onwards. It was widely regarded as the most perfect of languages – Ben Jonson speaks of it as 'queen of tongues' – and great emphasis was placed on learning to write it 'correctly', that is, in accordance with the usage of the great classical authors such as Cicero. It was taught in schools, and Latin grammar was used as a model for the description of all other languages – however dissimilar – despite the fact that it was no longer anyone's native tongue.

This had three direct effects on attitudes towards language. First, because of the emphasis on replicating the Latin of the 'best authors', people felt that there ought to be a fixed 'correct' form for any language, including English. Secondly, because Latin was primarily written and read, it led to the belief that the written language was in some sense superior to the spoken. Thirdly, even though our language is by no means a direct descendant of Latin, more like a great niece or nephew, English was viewed by many as having slipped from the classical purity of Latin by losing its endings. The idea that a language with a full set of endings for its nouns and verbs was superior to one without these appendages was very persistent. Even in the twentieth century, we find linguists forced to argue against this continuing irrational attachment to Latin: 'A linguist that insists on talking about the Latin type of morphology as though it were necessarily the high water mark of linguistic development is like the zoologist that sees in the organic world a huge conspiracy to evolve the race-horse or the Jersey cow,' wrote Edward Sapir in 1921.[21]

Against this background of admiration for a written language which appeared to have a fixed correct form and a full set of endings, there arose a widespread feeling that someone ought to adjudicate among the variant forms of English, and tell people what was 'correct'. The task was undertaken by Samuel Johnson, the son of a bookseller in Lichfield. Johnson, like many people of fairly humble origin, had an illogical reverence for his social betters. When he attempted to codify the English language in his famous dictionary he selected middle- and upper-class usage. When he said that he had 'laboured to refine our language to grammatical purity, and to clear it from colloquial barbarisms, licentious idioms, and irregular combinations',[22] he meant that he had in many instances pronounced against the spoken language of the lower classes, and in favour of the spoken and written forms of groups with social prestige. He asserted, therefore, that there were standards of correctness which should be adhered to, implying that these were already in use among certain social classes, and ought to be acquired by the others. Johnson's dictionary rightly had enormous influence, and its publication has been called 'the most important linguistic event of the eighteenth century'.[23] It was considered a worthwhile undertaking both by his contemporaries and later generations since it paid fairly close attention to actual usage, even if it was the usage of only a small proportion of speakers.

However, there were other eighteenth-century purists whose influence may have equalled that of Johnson, but whose statements and strictures were related not to usage, but to their own assumptions and prejudices. The most notable of these was Robert Lowth, Bishop of London. A prominent Hebraist and theologian, with fixed and eccentric opinions about language, he wrote *A Short Introduction to English Grammar* (1762) which had a surprising influence, perhaps because of his own high status. Indeed, many schoolroom grammars in use in this century have laws of 'good usage' which can be traced directly to Bishop Lowth's idiosyncratic pronouncements as to what was 'right' and what was 'wrong'. His grammar is bespattered with pompous notes in which he deplores the lamentable English of great writers. He set out to put matters right by laying down 'rules', which were often based on currently fashionable or even personal stylistic preferences. For example, contrary to general usage, he urged that prepositions at the end of sentences should be avoided:

> The Preposition is often separated from the Relative which it governs, and joined to the verb at the end of the Sentence . . . as, 'Horace is an author, whom I am much delighted with' . . . This is an Idiom which our language is strongly inclined to; it prevails in common conversation, and suits very well with the familiar style of writing; but the placing of the Preposition before the Relative is more graceful, as well as more per-spicuous; and agrees much better with the solemn and elevated style.[24]

As a result, the notion that it is somehow 'wrong' to end a sentence with a preposition is nowadays widely held. In addition, Lowth insisted on the pronoun *I* in phrases such as *wiser than I*, condemning lines of Swift such as 'she suffers hourly more than me', quite oblivious of the fact that many languages, English included, prefer a different form of the pronoun when it is detached from its verb: compare the French *plus sage que moi* 'wiser than me', not **plus sage que je*. In consequence, many people nowadays believe that a phrase such as *wiser than I* is 'better' than *wiser than me*. To continue, Lowth may have been the first to argue that a double negative is wrong, on the grounds that one cancels the other out. Those who support this point of view fail to realize that language is not logic or mathematics, and that the heaping up of negatives is very common in the languages of the world. It occurs frequently in Chaucer (and in other pre-eighteenth-century English authors). For example, in the Prologue to the *Canterbury Tales*, Chaucer heaps up negatives to emphasize the fact that the knight was never rude to anyone:

> He nevere yet no vileynye ne sayde
> In all his lyf unto no maner wight.
> He was a verray, parfit gentil knyght.[25]

Today, the belief that a double negative is wrong is perhaps the most widely accepted of all popular convictions about 'correctness'.

In brief, Lowth's influence was profound and pernicious because so many of his strictures were based on his own preconceived notions. In retrospect, it is quite astonishing that he should have felt so confident about his prescriptions. Did he believe that, as a bishop, he was divinely inspired? It is also curious that his dogmatic statements were so widely accepted among educated Englishmen. It seems that, as a prominent religious leader, no one questioned his authority.

We in the twentieth century are the direct descendants of this eighteenth-century puristic passion. As we have already noted, we still find statements very like those of Bishop Lowth in our books and newspapers, often reiterating the points he made – points which are still being drummed into the heads of the younger generation by parents and schoolteachers who misguidedly think they are handing over the essential prerequisites for speaking and writing 'good English'.

Not only are the strictures set on language often arbitrary, as in the case of many of Bishop Lowth's preferences, but, in addition, they cannot usually be said to 'purify' the language in any way. We have noted the journalist with a 'queasy distaste' for *the media is* (in place of the 'correct' form, *the media are*). To an impartial observer, the treatment of *media* as a singular noun might seem to be an advantage, not a sign of decay. Since most English plurals end in -*s*, it irons out an exception. Surely it is 'purer' to have all plurals ending in the same way? We find a similar complaint several centuries back over the word *chicken*. Once, *chick* was the singular, and *chicken* the plural, with -*en* as in *oxen*, *children*. In the course of time, these words became separated, and each was regarded as being singular: *chick* 'a baby hen' acquired the plural *chicks*, and *chicken* 'a young hen' acquired the plural *chickens*. Again, surely it is an advantage to smooth away exceptional plurals in this way? Yet we find a seventeenth-century grammarian stating, 'those who say *chicken* in the singular and *chickens* in the plural are completely wrong.'[26]

Purism, then, does not necessarily make language 'purer'. Nor does it always favour the older form, merely the most socially prestigious. A clear-cut example of this is the British dislike of the American form *gotten*, as in *he's gotten married*. Yet this is older than British *got*, and seen now in a few relic forms only such as *ill-gotten gains*.

In brief, the puristic attitude towards language – the idea that there is an absolute standard of correctness which should be maintained – has its origin in a natural nostalgic tendency in man, supplemented and intensified by social pressures. It is illogical, and impossible to pin down to any firm base. Purists behave as if there was a vintage year when language achieved a measure of excellence which we should all strive to maintain. In fact, there never was such a year. The language of Chaucer or Shakespeare's time was no better and no worse than that of our own – just different.

Of course, the fact that the puristic movement is wrong in the details it complains about does not prove that purists are wrong overall. Those who argue that language is decaying may be right for the wrong reasons, they may be entirely wrong, or they may be partially right and partially wrong. All we have discovered so far is that there are no easy answers, and that social prejudices simply cloud the issue.

Rules and grammars

Perhaps at this point we should make a distinction between the 'grammar' and 'rules' of Bishop Lowth and his followers, and those of linguists today. (By linguists, we mean people professionally concerned with linguistics, the study of language.) In Bishop Lowth's view, 'the principal design of a Grammar of any Language is to teach us to express ourselves with propriety in that Language, and to be able to judge of every phrase and form of construction, whether it be right or not. The plain way of doing this is to lay down rules.'[27] A grammar such as Lowth's, which lays down artificial rules in order to impose some arbitrary standard of 'correctness', is a **prescriptive** grammar, since it prescribes what people should, in the opinion of the writer, say. It may have relatively little to do with what people really say, a fact illustrated by a comment of Eliza Doolittle in Bernard Shaw's play *Pygmalion*: 'I don't want to talk grammar, I want to talk like a lady.' The artificial and constraining effect of Lowth's pseudo-rules might be summarized by lines from the Beatles' song 'Getting Better':

> I used to get mad at my school
> the teachers who taught me weren't cool
> holding me down, turning me round,
> filling me up with your rules ...

The grammars and rules of linguists, on the other hand, are not prescriptive but **descriptive**, since they describe what people actually say. For linguists, rules are not arbitrary laws imposed by an external authority, but a codification of subconscious principles or conventions followed by the speakers of a language. Note also that linguists regard the spoken and written forms of language as separate, related systems, and treat the spoken as primary.[28]

Let us consider the notion of **rules** (in this modern sense) more carefully. It is clear that it is impossible to list all the sentences of any human language. A language such as English does not have, say, 7,123,541 possible sentences which people gradually learn, one by one. Instead, the speakers of a language have a finite number of principles or 'rules' which enable them to understand and put together a potentially infinite number of sentences.

These rules vary from language to language. In English, for example, the sounds [b], [d], [e], can only occur in the order [bed], [deb], or [ebd] as in *ebbed*. *[bde], *[dbe] and *[edb] are all impossible, since we cannot begin words with [bd] or [db], or end them with [db], though these sequences are pronounceable. (An asterisk indicates a non-permitted sequence of sounds or words in the language concerned. Note also that sounds are conventionally indicated by square brackets.) Yet in ancient Greek, the sequence [bd] was allowable at the beginning of a word, as in *bdeluros* 'rascal', while a sequence [sl] as in *sleep* was not permitted.

Rules for permissible sequences exist also for segments of words, and words. In English, for instance, we find the recurring segments *love*, *-ing*, *-ly*. These can be combined to form *lovely*, *loving*, or *lovingly*, but not *ing-love*, *ly-love* or *love-ly-ing*. Similarly, you could say *Sebastian is eating peanuts*, but not *Sebastian is peanuts eating*, *Peanuts is eating Sebastian*, or *Eating is Sebastian peanuts* – though note that if the sentence was translated into a language such as Latin the words *Sebastian* and *peanuts* could occur in a greater variety of positions.

In brief, humans do not learn lists of utterances. Instead, they learn a number of principles or rules which they follow subconsciously. These are not pseudo-rules like Bishop Lowth's, but real ones which codify the actual patterns of the language. Although he uses the rules all the time, the average speaker cannot normally formulate them, any more than he could specify the muscles used when he rides a bicycle. In fact, in day-to-day life, we are so used to speaking and being understood that we are not usually aware of the rule-governed nature of our utterances. We only pause to think about it when the rules break down, or when someone uses rules which differ from our own, as when Alice in Looking-glass land tried to communicate with the Frog, whose subconscious language rules differed from her own. She asked him whose business it was to answer the door:

'To answer the door?' he said. 'What's it been asking of?'
'I don't know what you mean,' she said.
'I speaks English, doesn't I?' the Frog went on. 'Or
are you deaf?'

The sum total of the rules found in any one language is
known as a **grammar**, a term which is often used inter-
changeably by linguists to mean two different things: first,
the rules applied subconsciously by the speakers of a
language; secondly, a linguist's conscious attempt to
codify these rules. A statement such as, 'In English, you
normally put an -*s* on plural nouns', is an informal
statement of a principle that is known by the speakers of a
language, and is also likely to be expressed in a rather
more formal way in a grammar written by a linguist.
There are, incidentally, quite a number of differences
between a native speaker's grammar and a linguist's
grammar. Above all, they differ in completeness. All
normal native speakers of a language possess a far more
comprehensive set of rules than any linguist has yet been
able to specify, even though the former is not consciously
aware of his skill. No linguist has ever yet succeeded in
formulating a perfect grammar – an exhaustive summary
of the principles followed by the speakers of a language
when they produce and understand speech.

Note that this term **grammar** is normally used nowadays to cover the whole of a language: the **phonology**
(sound patterns), the **syntax** (word patterns), and the
semantics (meaning patterns). An important subdivision
within syntax is **morphology**, which deals with the organization of segments of words as in *kind-ness*, *kind-ly*,
un-kind, and so on.

The comprehensive scope of the word grammar sometimes causes confusion, since in some older books it is
used to mean only the syntax, and occasionally, only the
word endings. This has led to the strange claim that

English has practically no grammar at all – if this were really so, nobody would be able to speak it!

Grammars fluctuate and change over the centuries, and even within the lifetime of individuals. In this book, as we have explained, we shall be considering both how this happens, and why. Note that we shall be more interested in speakers' subconscious rules than in the addition and loss of single words. Vocabulary items tend to be added, replaced, or changed in meaning more rapidly than any other aspect 'of language. If we look through any big dictionary, we find numerous words which have totally disappeared from normal usage today, such as *scobberlotch* 'to loaf around doing nothing in particular', *ruddock* 'robin', *dudder* 'to deafen with noise', as well as an array of relatively new ones such as *atomizer, laser, transistorize*. Other words have changed their meaning in unpredictable ways. As Robin Lakoff has pointed out,[29] because of the decline in the employment of servants, the terms *master* and *mistress* are now used in rather different ways from their original meaning. *Master* now usually means 'to be supremely skilful in something', while *mistress*, on the other hand, often refers to a female lover:

He is a master of the intricacies of academic politics.
Rosemary refused to be Harry's mistress and returned to her husband.

The different ways in which these previously parallel words have changed is apparent if we try to substitute one for the other:

She is a mistress of the intricacies of academic politics.
Harry refused to be Rosemary's master and returned to his wife.

This particular change reflects not only a decline in the master or mistress to servant relationship, but also, according to Lakoff, the lowly status of women in our society.

The rapid turnover in vocabulary and the continual changes in the meaning of words are perhaps most interesting to a sociologist, since they often directly reflect social changes. A linguist is more likely to be interested in the less obvious aspects of language change, the sounds and syntax. It is therefore these more mysterious issues which will be the main concern of this book.

The chapters are organized into four main sections. Part 1, 'Preliminaries', deals mainly with the ways in which historical linguists obtain their evidence. Part 2, 'Implementation', explains *how* language change occurs, and Part 3, 'Causation', discusses possible reasons *why* change takes place. Part 4, 'Beginnings and Endings', looks at the role of child language and language disorders in relation to change, and examines how languages begin and end.

2 Collecting up Clues

How linguists piece together the evidence

> There was no light nonsense about Miss Blimber . . . She
> was dry and sandy with working in the graves of deceased
> languages. None of your live languages for Miss Blimber.
> They must be dead – stone dead – and then Miss Blimber
> dug them up like a Ghoul.
>
> Charles Dickens, *Dombey and Son*

A Faroese recipe in a recent cookbook explains how to
catch a puffin before you roast it.[1] Like a cook, a linguist
studying language change must first gather together his
basic ingredients. In his case, he must collect and piece
together the facts before he can interpret them. How does
he go about this?

There are basically two ways of collecting evidence,
which we may call the 'armchair method' and the 'tape-
recorder method' respectively. In the first, a linguist
studies the written documents of bygone ages, probably
sitting in a library, and in the second he slings a tape
recorder over his shoulder and studies change as it
happens. Both methods are important, and complement
one another. The armchair method enables him to follow
a large number of changes in outline over a long period,
whereas the tape-recorder method allows him to study a
relatively small amount of change in great detail.

The armchair method is the older, and the basic
techniques were laid down in the nineteenth century – as
is shown by the quotation above from Dickens' novel
Dombey and Son which was published in 1847–8. Let us
therefore deal with it first.

To a casual onlooker, sitting in a library studying old
documents sounds like an easy option. In practice, it

presents numerous problems. The data are inevitably variable in both quantity and quality, since some centuries and cultures are likely to be well-represented, others sparsely. Our knowledge of early Greek, for instance, might be rather different if Greece, like Egypt, had a sandy soil in which papyri can lie preserved for centuries. In all probability, the documents which survive will be from various regions, may represent a range of social classes, and are likely to have been written for different purposes. The letters of Queen Elizabeth I, for example, are rather different from the plays of William Shakespeare, even though they date from around the same time. A certain amount of the information will be damaged. Old tablets get chipped, and manuscripts are sometimes chewed by rats or coated in mildew. The data will be further obscured by the use of conventional orthography, which is often far from the spoken pronunciation. As the linguist de Saussure noted, 'Written forms obscure our view of language. They are not so much a garment as a disguise.'[2]

It is the task of the historical linguist to rectify, as far as he can, these shortcomings in the data. In brief, he must discover how the language of his documents was pronounced as a first priority, then go on to fill in the gaps by reconstructing what happened during periods for which he has no written records. Let us look at each of these tasks in turn.

Making old documents speak

Going behind the written form and making old documents 'speak' is a fascinating but time-consuming task. The reconstruction of pronunciation resembles the work of a detective, in that the linguist must seek out and piece together a vast assemblage of minute clues. He must follow the advice of Sherlock Holmes, who claims that, 'It has long been an axiom of mine that the little things are infinitely the most important.'[3] As in detective work, each individual piece of evidence is of little value on its own. It is the cumulative effect which counts. When a linguist finds several clues all pointing in the same direction, he can be more confident that his reconstruction is a plausible one.

The type of clue he uses varies from language to language. English is perhaps simpler to deal with than a number of others because it traditionally uses rhyme in its poetry:

> You spotted snakes with double tongue,
> Thorny hedge-hogs, be not seen;
> Newts, and blind-worms, do no wrong;
> Come not near our fairy queen.[4]

These lines from Shakespeare's *A Midsummer Night's Dream* suggest that in the sixteenth century, *tongue* rhymed with *wrong*, rather than with *rung* as it would today. By itself, this piece of evidence is unconvincing, since Shakespeare may have been using poetic licence and forcing words to rhyme which did not in fact do so. Or his pronunciation may have been an old or idiosyncratic one. Or he may have been mimicking a French accent, or *tongue* might have had alternative pronunciations. On the other hand, it may be the word *wrong* which has changed, not *tongue*. Whatever the truth of the matter, this is the type of clue which a linguist must seize and check up on. He will look for further examples, and for other types of corroborating evidence. (In this case, the rhyme is supported by a play on words between *tongues* and *tongs* in *Twelfth Night*.[5])

Puns provide similar information to rhymes: for example, in Shakespeare's *The Merchant of Venice*, Shylock starts to sharpen his knife on his shoe, preparing to cut a pound of flesh away from his victim's breast. At this point a bystander says:

> Not on thy sole, but on thy soul, harsh Jew,
> Thou mak'st the knife keen[6]

indicating that the words *sole* and *soul* were pronounced similarly by the late-sixteenth century (their spelling shows they once differed). Puns are particularly useful when they occur in languages where rhymes are not normal, such as classical Latin. For instance, the Roman general Marcus Crassus was preparing to go on a military expedition which later proved disastrous. As he was about to board his ship, a fig-seller approached him saying *Cauneas* 'figs from Caunea'. Cicero, the narrator of this episode, pointed out that Crassus was foolish to have proceeded with his expedition, since the fig-seller was uttering a cryptic warning and was really saying *Cave ne eas* 'Don't go'.[7] The confusion of *cauneas* with *cave ne eas* shows clearly that Latin *v* was indistinguishable from *u* at this point in time, and that unstressed vowels were often omitted.

Representations of animal noises may also be informative. In some fragments of ancient Greek comedy, the bleating of sheep is represented by the sequence $\beta\hat{\eta}$ $\beta\hat{\eta}$.[8] A modern Greek would read this as *vee-vee* [vi: vi:]. Since sheep are unlikely to have changed their basic *baa-baa* cry in two thousand years, we may be fairly confident that the ancient and modern Greek pronunications of the sequence $\beta\hat{\eta}$ $\beta\hat{\eta}$ are rather different.

Social climbers can also inadvertently give us clues. In the first century BC the Roman poet Catullus laughs gently at a man who said *hinsidias* 'hambush' instead of the correct *insidias* 'ambush' – a word which had never had an *h*.[9] This indicates that *h* was still pronounced in fashionable circles, but had been lost in less prestigious types of speech. Consequently, social climbers attempted to insert it, but sometimes made mistakes, and added an aspirate where one never existed. A similar example occurs in Charles Dickens' *Pickwick Papers*, when Mr Pickwick's servant Sam Weller speaks of 'gas miscroscopes of hextra power'.[10]

Spelling mistakes may provide useful information. The Romans, for example, had an official known as a *consul* and another called a *censor*. These titles were sometimes misspelt on inscriptions as *cosul* and *cesor*, indicating that the *n* was probably omitted in casual speech.[11]

Indirect clues of the type we have discussed so far can sometimes be supplemented by statements from old grammarians. There are a number of ancient treatises on language in existence, perhaps more than most people realize. Some are vague, but others informative. For example, in the sixteenth century, a court official named John Hart wrote a fairly clear account of the English pronunciation of his time, noting among other things that *a* was produced 'with a wyde opening of the mouth as when a man yauneth',[12] indicating that *a* in his time was probably similar to that in the standard British English pronunciation of *father*.

Detailed accounts exist also of ancient Greek and Latin pronunciation. Read the following phonetic description, and try to work out the sound specified by the Roman grammarian Victorinus: 'We produce the letter by pressing the lower lip on the upper teeth. The tongue is turned back towards the roof of the mouth, and the sound is accompanied by a gentle puff of breath.' This is a fairly accurate description of the pronunciation of the sound [f].[13]

The clues mentioned above are only a selection of the total possible ones. We have also ignored the extra problems which arise when the linguist is dealing with a syllabary – a writing system which uses one sign per syllable – or how a linguist might attempt to decipher an unknown script. But the general picture is clear: the linguist, like a detective or an archaeologist, patiently searches for and pieces together fragmentary clues. Bit by minute bit, he builds up a complete picture. When he feels that he has satisfactorily reconstructed the pronunciation of the words in his documents, he can proceed to the next stage – the filling in of gaps. At this point, he attempts to reconstruct what the language was like during the periods for which he has no written evidence.

Filling the gaps

There are certain areas of scholarship, early Greek history is one and Roman law is another, where the scantiness of the evidence sets a special challenge to the disciplined mind. It is a game with very few pieces where the skill of the player lies in complicating the rules. The isolated and uneloquent fact must be exhibited within a tissue of hypothesis subtle enough to make it speak, and it was the weaving of this tissue which fascinated Ducane.

Ducane is a character in Iris Murdoch's novel *The Nice and the Good* and his interest was in Roman Law. But the quotation also applies particularly well to anyone involved in piecing together linguistic evidence from old documents.

Essentially, a linguist needs to fill two kinds of gap. On the one hand, she must push back our knowledge of the language to a point prior to that of our first written records. On the other hand she must bridge the gaps between documents. In this way, she may build up a picture of the development of a language over a span of hundreds or even thousands of years, as in Figure 2.1.

Pushing back the past is a topic which has long been the concern of linguists. In the nineteenth century, scholars regarded the task of reconstructing the hypothetical language spoken by our Indo-European ancestors some five or six thousand years ago as one of major importance, so much so that a number of people today have the mistaken impression that such a preoccupation is the backbone of linguistics. Nowadays it is simply one smallish branch of the subject.

The hypothetical forefather of a group of related languages is known as a **proto-language**. Proto-Indo-European, for example, is the presumed parent language from which a number of present-day languages such as Greek, German, English, Welsh, Hindi etc. subsequently developed. Building up a picture of a proto-language is

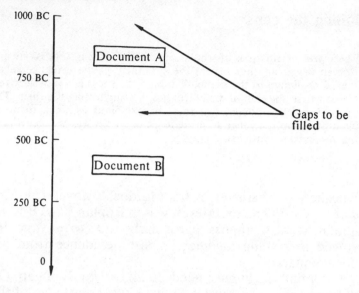

Fig. 2.1 : Filling in the gaps

known as **comparative historical linguistics**, because conclusions are reached by comparing a number of different languages. Note that the old name for the subject, comparative philology, tends to be avoided because of the confusion it creates in America and Europe where 'philology' more usually refers to the scholarly study of literary texts.

In brief, comparative reconstruction involves comparing corresponding words from a number of related languages and drawing conclusions about their common ancestor, in the same way that one might be able to draw up a reasonable physical description of a man or woman from a close examination of his or her grandchildren.

This type of comparison relies on two basic assumptions: the first is that language is essentially arbitrary in the sense that there is no intrinsic connection between a linguistic symbol and what it stands for, apart from a few onomatopoeic words such as *bang*, *splash*, *plop*. For example, there is no deep reason for the word *squid* to represent a particular type of marine animal described by dictionaries as a 'ten-armed cephalopod', since there is no essential 'squiddiness' in the sound sequence [skwɪd]. It is a purely conventional label, as are the names for this animal in other languages, such as *calmar* (French), *tauka* (Melanesian Pidgin).

The second basic assumption of comparative historical linguistics is that sound changes are to a large extent consistent or 'regular' rather than haphazard. Just as tulips which are planted in the same area and exposed to similar soil and weather conditions tend to flower and wither at around the same time, so a sound change is likely to affect comparable instances of the same sound within the dialect affected. Take the word *leisure*. There used to be a genuine [s] in the middle of this word which changed first to [z] and then to its present-day sound [ʒ]. But this was not an isolated happening, limited to one word: the change also occurred in *pleasure*, *treasure*, *measure*, and so on.

These basic assumptions of arbitrariness and regularity allow us to make the following deduction. If we find consistent sound correspondences between words with similar meanings in languages where we can rule out the possibility of borrowing, the correspondences cannot be due to chance. We therefore infer that the languages concerned are so-called 'daughter languages' descended from one 'parent'. For example, we consistently find *f* in English where Latin has *p* in words with similar meaning such as *father*:*pater*, *foot*:*pedem*, *fish*:*pisces*, and so on. There is no evidence of a Latin-English cultural bond. When the Romans first came to Britain, the woad-painted natives they found did not yet speak English, which was brought from across the Channel at a later date. So we can eliminate borrowing as the source of the regular *f*:*p* correspondence. We conclude therefore that Latin and English are both descended from the same parent, which must have existed at some earlier age. Of course, one single set of correspondences, such as the $f:p$ set, is too frail a foundation on which to set any firm conclusions, so we must back this up with others such as $s:s$ in *six*:*sex*, *seven*:*septem*, *salt*:*sel*, *sun*:*sol*, and $t:d$ in *two*:*duo*, *ten*:*decem*, *tooth*:*dens* and so on. The more correspondences we find, the more certain we become that the languages concerned are genetically related.

When we have assembled correspondences from two or more related languages, we can begin to draw conclusions about the parent from which they sprang. We follow methods similar to any other type of historian. Suppose we were reconstructing the physical characteristics of grandparents from a group of grandchildren. We might begin by considering eye colour. If we found that all the grandchildren had blue eyes except one, we would probably suggest that the grandparents had blue eyes too, and would discount the odd one out. The only thing that would alter our decision might be the knowledge that we had proposed something physically impossible, but in this case, there seems no reason to change our hypothesis, since blue-eyed grandparents could quite easily have grandchildren with brown or blue eyes. Linguistic reconstruction works in the same way. We take the majority verdict as our major guideline, and then check that we have not proposed anything that is phonetically implausible. For example, a number of Indo-European languages have s at the beginning of certain words: English has *six*, *seven*, *sun*, *salt*, *sow* 'female pig'. Latin has *sex*, *septem*, *sol*, *sel*, *sus*, and so on. Greek, however, has an h in place of the expected s, with *hex*, *hepta*, *helios*, *hals*, *hus*. Since Greek is the odd man out, we conclude that the original sound was probably s, and that Greek changed an original s to h. We confirm that s to h is a fairly common development (and note that the reverse, h to s is unheard of). Our hypothesis can therefore stand. We shall of course look for further corroborative evidence, and amend our theory if we find any counter evidence.

If a majority verdict leads us to a conclusion that is phonetically improbable, we would revise our original suggestion. For example, faced with the Spanish, Italian and Sardinian words for 'smoke' which are *umo*, *fumo*, and *ummu* respectively, the majority verdict would lead us to suggest that the word originally began with the vowel *u*, and that Italian had inserted an *f* at the beginning. However, we are unable to find other examples of *f* spontaneously appearing in front of a vowel, though we note that the disappearance of *f* at the beginning of a word is common, usually with an intermediate stage of *h* (*f* → *h* → zero). Here, then, phonetic probability overrules the majority verdict, and we propose *f* as the sound at the beginning of the word 'smoke' at an earlier stage – an assumption we can in this case check, since we know that Latin, the ancestor of the three languages in question had a word *fumus* 'smoke'.

The examples above are straightforward ones, but in practice the situation is often messier. Usually the behaviour of a sound varies, depending on its position in a word. Or we might need to reconstruct a sound which did not occur in any of the daughter languages. Or an influx of invaders speaking a totally different language might have obscured the situation. Or variant forms might represent different dialects of the parent tongue. The linguist must be aware of all these possibilities, and must constantly be on the lookout for new evidence and be prepared to revise his hypotheses about the proto-language. Certainty is impossible, and there are subtleties and complications in the use of comparative reconstruction which cannot be discussed here. But the basic principles of majority verdict followed by a probability check are likely to remain the main methodological foundations of this type of reconstruction.

The method has been applied in most detail to the Indo-European language family, and we now know quite a lot about the probable appearance of Proto-Indo-European, the ancestor of a large number of Indian,

Iranian and European languages, which probably flourished around 2500 BC. More recently, useful work has been done on other language families such as Sino-Tibetan (which includes Chinese), Semitic (which includes Hebrew and Arabic) and various American-Indian groups.

We should note, incidentally, that reconstruction does not lead back to any kind of 'primitive language'. Poo-Bah in *The Mikado* claimed that he could trace his ancestry back 'to a proto plasmal primordial atomic globule'. The same is not true of reconstruction. Reconstructed Indo-European is a fully-fledged language, not a system of primordial grunts.

Comparative reconstruction has proved most useful in the reconstruction of sound systems and inflectional endings. More recently, scholars have attempted to draw some tentative conclusions about syntax. For example, in the earliest documents most Indo-European languages have objects preceding their verbs. That is, simple sentences have the order *Pigs apples eat* rather than *Pigs eat apples*. Majority verdict in this case leads us to suspect that verbs were normally placed at the end of sentences in the parent language.

In the past few years, however, a more ingenious and more controversial way of reconstructing syntax has begun to be developed. This is known as **typological reconstruction** and is based on the insight that languages can be divided into a number of basic types, each with its own set of characteristics. We have known for a long time that it is possible to divide humans physically into a number of racial types – Caucasian, Negroid, and so on, and can list the characteristics associated with each type. Recently, linguists have realized that we can do the same for languages. English, for example, can be categorized as a verb-object (VO) language, since it places its object after the verb, as in *Bears eat honey*. One fairly predictable characteristic of VO languages is that they place extra or auxiliary verbs befor. 'he main verb, as in *Bears may eat* *honey*. The reverse happens in object-verb (OV) languages such as Turkish, Hindi, Japanese, which place auxiliaries after the verb, and say, as it were, *Bears honey eat may*.

If, therefore, we are able partially to reconstruct the syntax of a language by means of comparative reconstruction, we can then infer more detailed knowledge about it by assigning it to its probable language type. Our knowledge of the characteristics associated with its type will allow us to predict facts for which we have no direct evidence.

As noted above, this type of reconstruction is still controversial. Problems arise because few languages seem to represent 'pure' types – most are a mixture with one type predominating. In addition, people are still arguing about what the 'pure' types should look like, or even whether we are looking at the right kind of criteria when we assign languages to types. But taken alongside other evidence, typological reconstruction allows us to push back further into the past than we otherwise could.

In addition to comparative and typological reconstruction, there is a third method of pushing back the past, known as **internal reconstruction**. This involves making a detailed study of one language at a single point in time, and deducing facts about a previous state of that language. Essentially, we assume that irregularities in structure are likely to have been brought about by language change. We therefore try to peel these away, in order to reconstruct an earlier, more regular state of affairs.

Let us give an example. Consider the chorus of the Tom Lehrer song, 'When you are old and grey':

An awful *debility*, a lessened *utility*,
   a loss of *mobility* is a strong *possibility*.
In all *probability*, I'll lose my *virility*,
   and you your *fertility* and *desirability*.
And this *liability* of total *sterility*
   will lead to *hostility* and a sense of *futility*.
So let's act with *agility* while we still have *facility*.
   for we'll soon reach *senility* and lose the *ability*.

This song shows clearly that abstract nouns ending in -*ity* are a common formation in English, and we could add dozens more to the above list, such as *purity, obscurity, serenity, virginity, profanity, obscenity, sanity*, and so on. We note further that many of these nouns in -*ity* are paired with adjectives, as in *mobile/mobility, possible/ possiblity, pure/purity, serene/serenity, sane/sanity* and numerous others. We see that a number of these nouns are formed simply by adding -*ity* on to the end of the adjective, as in *virgin/virginity, pure/purity, passive/ passivity*. In others, however, the vowels in the noun and corresponding adjective differ, as in *senile/senility, sane/ sanity, serene/serenity*.

Why do we find this difference? Why can we not simply add -*ity* on to the adjective for all of them? Following the principles of internal reconstruction, we suggest that this was the situation at some unspecified time in the past, and that the pairs which fail to match up have undergone change. Of course, we do not know whether it is the adjective which has undergone change, or the form to which -*ity* is attached, or both. As in external reconstruction, we use phonetic probability to guide us in our reconstruction, as well as (in this case) the clues given by the spelling. The most plausible suggestion is that a pair such as *serene/serenity* originally had [e:] in the second syllable, rather like the vowel in *bed* somewhat lengthened. [e:] then changed to [i:] in *serene* [səri:n], and was shortened to [e] in *serenity* [sərenɪtɪ]. In English we have copious written records, and can check this hypothesis. Sure enough, we find a situation in Middle English where *serene/serenity* both had [e:] in the second syllable. Similarly, pairs such as *profane/profanity* both had a common vowel [a:], rather like the *a* in *father*, and pairs such as *hostile/hostility* had a common [i:] like the vowel in the second syllable of *machine* – so confirming our reconstructed forms.[14]

Our second example of internal reconstruction is a less obvious one, and relates to the sounds [θ] as in *thin* and [ð] as in *then*. If we examine the distribution of these sounds in modern English, we find a curious imbalance. [ð] hardly ever occurs at the beginning of words, apart from a smallish group of related words such as *the, this, that, those, then, there*. Yet it is very common inside words, as in *father, mother, feather, heather, weather, bother, rather*, and so on. The [θ] situation is just the opposite. There are numerous words beginning with [θ], such as *thick, thin, thigh, thank, think, thaw, thimble, thief, thorn, thistle*, and many others. Yet [θ] hardly ever occurs in the middle of words. It is possible to find a few scattered examples such as *breathy, pithy, toothy*, but not many. Why? This uneven distribution suggests that at an earlier stage of English, [θ] and [ð] were variants of the same basic sound, which was pronounced as [θ] at the beginning of a word, and [ð] inside it – as is now thought to have been the case.[15]

This type of reconstruction is not really needed for a language such as English for which we already have copious data. It is indispensable, however, in cases where we have no earlier written records, or where there is a big gap in the evidence, especially as we can sometimes work backwards for quite a long way. Once we have peeled off one layer, we are then likely to find new irregularities revealed.

Inevitably, the method has problems, especially if we are dealing with a language such as Chinese which tends not to have neat pairs of related words such as *mobile/mobility*. In addition, we are in danger of getting our chronology very muddled, since we cannot always tell how long ago the pairs we are working from formed a single unit. Nevertheless, internal reconstruction is a valuable tool if no others are available.

When we put together the three methods of reconstruction outlined in this chapter – comparative historical, typological and internal – and combine them with careful study of the surviving texts, we find that we are able to follow the development of a number of languages for a period of up to 5000 years. The combined efforts of scholars in the field of reconstruction over the past 150 years means that we now have a very large body of information about possible changes and long-term trends in languages. In fact, we have more outline data on sound change over the centuries than could possibly ever be handled by one linguist. What we *are* short of, are detailed records of language changes actually in progress. Let us consider why this is, and how we go about collecting such data.

3 *Charting the Changes*

How linguists study changes in progress

> The crisis consists precisely in the fact that the old is dying
> and the new cannot be born; in this interregnum a great
> variety of morbid symptoms appear.
> Antonio Gramsci, *Prison Notebooks*

Until relatively recently, the majority of linguists were
convinced that language change was unobservable. Most
of them simply accepted that it happened, but could never
be pinpointed. A popular assumption was that language
change was a continuous but very slow process, like the
rotation of the earth, or the creeping up of wrinkles, or
the opening of flowers. It happened so slowly and over so
many decades that it was quite impossible to detect its
occurrence. You could only look at it beforehand and
afterwards, and realize it had happened, just as you might
glance at a watch at four o'clock, and then at ten past
four. You could note that ten minutes had passed by, but
you would probably not have seen the hands actually
moving. Leonard Bloomfield, sometimes called 'the
father of American linguistics', stated in 1933 that 'the
process of linguistic change has never been directly
observed – we shall see that such observation, with our
present facilities, is inconceivable'.[1] As recently as 1958,
another influential American linguist, Charles Hockett,
claimed that 'No one has yet observed sound change; we
have only been able to detect it via its consequences. . . .
A more nearly direct observation would be theoretically
possible, if impractical, but any ostensible report of such
an observation so far must be discredited.'[2]

Why should intelligent men who spent their whole lives working on language be so convinced that change was unobservable? The answer is simply that they did not know where to look. They looked in the wrong direction because they uncritically adopted certain methodological guidelines laid down for the study of language at the beginning of this century.

In the early twentieth century, many linguists consciously turned their backs on the 'absurdities of reasoning'[3] and non-rigorous approach of their nineteenth century predecessors. They attempted to lay down a 'scientific' framework for the study of language which led to the making of a number of useful, but oversimplified, distinctions.

One much praised methodological principle was the strict separation of **diachronic** linguistics, the study of language change, from **synchronic** linguistics, the study of the state of a language at a given point in time. This principle dated from the time of Ferdinand de Saussure (1857–1913), who has been labelled 'the father of modern linguistics'. His statements about the necessity of separating the two aspects of linguistics were dogmatic and categorical: 'The opposition between the two viewpoints – synchronic and diachronic – is absolute and allows of no compromise'.[4] He likened the two viewpoints to cuts through the trunk of a tree (see Figure 3.1). Either one made a horizontal cut, and examined a language at a single point in time, or one made a vertical cut, and followed the development of selected items over the course of a number of years.

For most of the twentieth century, synchronic linguistics was considered to be prior to diachronic linguistics. A historical linguist was expected to gather together descriptions of a language at various points in time, relying to a large extent on the previous work of synchronic linguists. Then he studied the changes which had taken place by comparing the various synchronic states. He behaved somewhat like a photographer trying to work out a

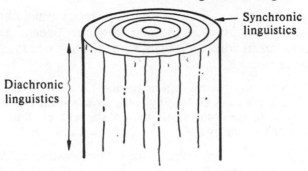

Fig. 3.1 : The tree-trunk analogy of Saussure

continuous sequence of events from a series of separate snapshots – on the face of it, a sensible enough procedure. The problem was simply this: linguists making the synchronic descriptions were, without realizing it, simply leaving out those aspects of the description that were essential for an understanding of language change. How did this happen? Let us consider why they unwittingly omitted the crucial evidence.

The missing evidence

In the first chapter, we noted that there is a set of underlying rules which people who know a language subconsciously follow, the sum total of which constitutes a grammar. This statement implies that it is, in principle, possible for a linguist to write a perfect grammar, to formulate a complete set of rules which will account for all the well-formed sentences of a language and reject all the ill-formed ones. In practice, this optimistic aim faces a number of problems involving **language variation** on the one hand, and **language fuzziness** on the other.

Consider, first, the question of language variation. The most obvious type is geographical variation. Everybody is aware that people from different geographical areas are likely to display differences in their speech, as Ivy, a character in John Steinbeck's novel *The Grapes of Wrath*, points out:

'Ever'body says words different,' said Ivy. 'Arkansas folks says 'em different, and Oklahomy folks says 'em different. And we seen a lady from Massachusetts, an' she said 'em differentest of all. Couldn' hardly make out what she was sayin'.'

This type of variation does not present us with any insuperable problems. We simply note that the grammatical rules of a language are likely to alter slightly from region to region, and we then try to specify what these alterations are – though we must not expect abrupt changes between areas, more a gradual shifting with no clear-cut breaks.

Parallel to geographical variation, we find social variation. As we move from one social class to another, we are likely to come across the same type of alterations as we noted from region to region, only this time co-existing within a single area. Once again, this second type of variation does not surprise us, and we simply need to specify the minor rule alterations which occur between the different strata of society. Here also we are likely to find a certain amount of overlap between the different classes.

These fairly straightforward types of variation are represented in Figure 3.2 which shows social variation as a

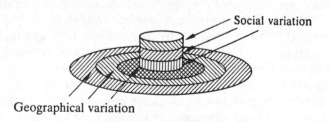

Fig. 3.2 : Social and geographical dialect variation

number of slightly different dialects heaped on top of one
another, and geographical variation as a number of
slightly different dialects spread out side by side.

So far, so good. More problematical, however, are the
variations in style which exist within the speech of individual speakers. These variations have somewhat fac-
etiously been likened to the two clocks which are reputed
to exist on Ballyhough railway station, which disagree by
some six minutes. One day a helpful Englishman pointed
this fact out to the porter, whose reply was 'Faith Sir, if
they was to tell thé same time, why should we be having
two of them?'[5]

These stylistic variations are not, in fact, as random as
the above anecdote suggests. Almost every speaker of a
language is likely to alter his speech to fit the casualness or
formality of the occasion, though he is often unaware of
doing so. For example, in informal situations a London
schoolboy will drop his aitches, alter the *t* in the middle of
words such as *football*, or the end of the word *what* to a
'glottal stop' – a stoppage of outgoing breath with no actual *t* pronounced – and change the *l* at the end of a word
such as *thistle, drizzle* into a *u*-like sound. But in an
interview with his headmaster, or a visit to a fastidious
grandmother, the schoolboy is likely to pronounce the
words more slowly and carefully, and to put in the
consonants omitted in casual speech. Variations occur not
only in pronunciation, but also in syntax and vocabulary.
Contractions such as *wanna, I'd, we've, ain't* are likely to
be common in casual situations, but replaced by *want to, I
would, we have, I haven't* in more formal ones. A man
might say 'Shut up and sit down' to his young son when he
wants him to sit down and eat, but 'Gentlemen, please be
seated' to colleagues at a formal dinner. Or, to take
another example, the linguist Robin Lakoff points out
that in some social situations euphemisms are common,
whereas in scientific literature they are completely out of
place.[6] She notes that at a certain type of party, someone
might conceivably say 'Harold has gone to the little boys'

room', whereas in the anthropological literature, we might find a sentence such as: 'When the natives of Mbanga wish to defecate, first they find a large pineapple leaf.' It would, however, be very strange to find an anthropologist saying: 'When the natives of Mbanga wish to use the little boys' room, they first find a large pineapple leaf', or to find someone announcing at a party that: 'Harold has gone to defecate' unless her intention is to shock or antagonize the other partygoers.

In brief, it is normal for a speaker to have a variety of different forms in his repertoire, and to vary them according to the needs of the occasion. It is difficult to reconcile this fluctuation with the notion that there is a fixed set of rules which speakers follow. It is not surprising, therefore, that many conscientious linguists felt it was their duty to ignore this 'purely social' variation and concentrate on the more rigid 'central core' of the language.

Language fuzziness received similar treatment. Consider the following sentences, and try to decide whether each is a 'normal' or 'good' English sentence.

> I saw a man scarlet in the face.
> Who did the postman bring the letter?
> Did you see anyone not pretty in Honolulu?
> He promised me to come.
> He donated the charity ten dollars.

What is your opinion? Most people would judge them to be borderline cases, and make comments such as, 'They sound a bit odd, but I can't really lay my finger on what's wrong.' 'I wouldn't say them myself, but they're probably possible.' 'I don't think they are really English, but I'm not sure.' So, are these sentences well-formed or not? If a linguist is writing a set of rules which distinguish well-formed from ill-formed sentences, he needs to make a decision about cases such as those above. How should he do this when the speakers of the language seem unable to judge? Once again, it seemed best to many linguists writing grammars to deal first and foremost with the clear-cut cases. In the opinion of many, borderline messiness was perhaps unsolvable, and so best left alone.

To summarize, descriptive linguists aim to write a set of rules which tell us which sequences of a language are permissible, and which not. When faced with social fluctuations and unsolvable fuzziness, the majority of linguists have, in the past, made the understandable decision to concentrate on the clear-cut cases and ignore the messy bits. 'All grammars leak,' said the insightful anthropologist-linguist Edward Sapir in 1921.[7] Yet, for the first two-thirds of the twentieth century, most linguists tried to pretend that grammars could be watertight. Since diachronic linguists based their studies of language change on these watertight grammars, it is not surprising that they failed to identify changes in progress, which are signalled by the frayed edges of languages. These frayed edges must be examined, not snipped away and tidied up. To return to the words of Gramsci, quoted at the beginning of this chapter, these are the 'morbid symptoms' which occur when 'the old is dying and the new cannot be born'. Let us now go on to consider how these morbid symptoms have been charted in recent years.

Charting fluctuations

In the past twenty years, linguists have realized that language change *is* observable, provided one knows where to look. The pioneer in this field is William Labov, an American at the University of Pennsylvania. Labov recognized clearly one important fact: the variation and fuzziness which so many linguists tried to ignore are quite often indications that changes are in progress.

This insight is not, of course, entirely new, and the observation that changes involve periods of fluctuation occurs in several places in the literature – even though no one had paid much attention to it. Labov's essential contribution to linguistics is that he showed that variation and fuzziness are amenable to strict observation and statistical analysis.

Consider the fluctuating *r* in New York speech. Sometimes New Yorkers pronounce an *r* in words such as *car*, *bear*, *beard* and sometimes they do not. Early reports of the phenomenon suggested that the insertion or omission of *r* was a purely chance affair, with no rhyme or reason to it. The following report is typical: 'The speaker hears both types of pronunciation about him all the time, both seem almost equally natural to him, and it is a matter of pure chance which one comes to his lips.'[8] Labov rejected this notion of randomness. He had a hunch that the presence or absence of *r* would not be mere chance, but would be correlated with social status. Let us consider how he set about testing this hunch and how he developed methodology for dealing with linguistic fluctuation in an objective and reliable way.

Labov made a preliminary check on his hunch that New York *r* was related to social status by an ingenious and amusing method. He checked the speech of sales people in a number of New York stores.[9] Sociologists have found that salesgirls in large department stores subconsciously mimic their customers, particularly when the customers have relatively high social status. Labov hoped, therefore, that if he picked three Manhattan department stores from the top, middle, and bottom of the price and fashion range, that the sales people would reflect this social pattern in the pronunciation or non-pronunciation of *r* in their speech. Therefore, he picked first Saks Fifth Avenue, which is near the centre of the high-fashion shopping district. It is a spacious store with carpeted floors, and on the upper floors very few goods on display. His second store was the middle-ranking Macy's, which is regarded as a middle-class, middle-priced store. His third was Klein's, a cheap store seemingly cluttered with goods, not far from the Lower East Side – a notoriously poor area. Compared with Saks, Klein's is a 'maze of annexes, sloping concrete floors, low ceilings – it has the maximum amount of goods displayed at the least possible expense.'[10] Comparative prices also showed the difference: women's coats in Saks cost on average over three times as much as women's coats in Klein's, while prices in Macy's were about twice as high as those in Klein's.

The technique used was surprisingly simple. The interviewer pretended to be a customer. He approached one of the staff and asked to be directed to a particular department, which was located on the fourth floor. For example, 'Excuse me, where are the women's shoes?' When the answer was given, the interviewer then leaned forward as if he had not heard properly, and said 'Excuse me?' This would normally lead to a repetition of the words 'Fourth floor', only this time spoken more carefully and with emphatic stress.

As soon as he had received these answers, the interviewer would then hastily move out of sight and make a note of the pronunciation, recording also other factors such as the sex, approximate age, and race of the shop assistant. On the fourth floor, of course, the interviewer asked a slightly different question: 'Excuse me, what floor is this?' In this way, a total of 264 interviews was carried out in the three stores.

As Labov had hypothesized, there was an interesting variation in the use of *r* in each store: the overall percentage of *r* inclusion was higher in Saks than in Macy's and higher in Macy's than in Klein's. And interestingly, the overall percentage of *r* inclusion was higher on the *upper* floors at Saks than the ground floor. The ground floor of Saks looks very like Macy's, with crowded counters and a considerable amount of merchandise on display. But the upper floors of Saks are far more spacious: there are long vistas of empty carpeting, and on the floors devoted to high fashion, there are models who display the individual garments to the customers. Receptionists are stationed at strategic points to screen out the casual spectators from the serious buyers.

So far, then Labov's hunch was confirmed. His results suggested that there is social stratification in New York which is reflected in language: the higher socio-economic groups tend to insert *r* in words such as *beard*, *bear*, *car*, *card*, while the lower social groups tend to omit it. But what evidence is there that an actual *change* is taking place?

An interesting pointer that a change was occurring was the difference between the casual speech and the emphatic speech in the data from Klein's. At Klein's, there was a significantly higher proportion of *r*s inserted in the more careful, emphatic repetition of 'fourth floor', than in the original casual response to the interviewer's query. It seemed as if these assistants had at least two styles of speech: a casual style, in which they did not consciously think about what they said and a more careful, formal style in which they tried to insert elements which they felt were socially desirable. Labov suggested, then, that the reinsertion of *r* was an important characteristic of a new prestige pattern which was being superimposed upon the native New York pattern. This is supported by descriptions of New York speech in the early part of the century, which suggests that *r* was virtually absent at this time – a fact observable in films made in New York in the 1930s.

In the next chapter we shall consider where such changes start, and how they spread. We shall also be looking at changes which are not moving in the direction of a socially acceptable pronunciation. In this chapter we shall continue to concern ourselves with Labov's methodology: how he observed and charted language variation.

Labov's successful department-store survey encouraged him to make a more detailed survey of pronunciation habits in New York City. He examined a number of other fluctuating sounds, or **linguistic variables**, as they are usually called. Apart from a further analysis of *r*, he looked at the sounds at the beginning of *the*, *this*, *that*, which in New York are sometimes pronounced *de*, *dis*, *dat*. He also scrutinized the wide range of vowels used in

words such as *dog, coffee, more, door, bad, back*. In order
to do this, he conducted long interviews with a balanced
population sample whose social position, age, ethnic
group, occupation and geographic history were known.
But he faced one major problem. His department-store
survey showed that he needed to elicit a *range* of speech
styles from each person. Often, it was the variation
between styles which indicated that a change was taking
place. How should he set about eliciting these different
styles?

Samples of careful speech were relatively easy to
obtain. Labov and his assistants interviewed selected
individuals, and asked them about themselves and their
use of language. Since the interviewers were well-
educated strangers, those interviewed tended to speak
fairly carefully. The speech used was less formal than in a
job interview, but more formal than in casual conversation with the family. Samples of even more careful speech
were obtained by asking people to read a prose passage,
and of extra careful speech by asking them to read word
lists.

The chief difficulty arose with obtaining samples of
casual speech. As Labov notes: 'We must somehow
become witnesses to the everyday speech which the
informant will use as soon as the door is closed behind us:
the style in which he argues with his wife, scolds his
children, or passes the time of day with his friends. The
difficulty of the problem is considerable.'[11]

Labov found there was no one method which he could
use. Within the interview situation, he devised one ingenious way of eliciting casual style, and this was to say to
people: 'Have you ever been in a situation where you
thought you were in serious danger of being killed –
where you thought to yourself, "This is it."?' As the
narrators became emotionally involved in remembering
and recounting a dramatic incident of this type, they often
moved without realizing it into a more casual style of
speech. For example, nineteen-year-old Eddie had been

reserved and careful in his replies until he described how he had been up a ship's mast in a strong wind, when the rope tied round him to stop him from falling had parted, and left him 'just hanging there by my fingernails'. At this point, his breathing became heavy and irregular, his voice began to shake, sweat appeared on his forehead, small traces of nervous laughter appeared in his speech, and his pronunciation changed noticeably: 'I never prayed to God so fast and so hard in my life . . . . Well, I came out all right . . . . Well, the guys came up and they got me . . . . Yeah, I came down, I couldn't hold a pencil in my hand. I couldn't touch nuttin'. I was shaking like a leaf.'[12]

In another interview, a woman named Rose described a road accident she had had in her childhood. Thirteen of them had piled into one car, a wheel fell off, and the car turned over. As she recounted the incident, her speech became rapid and colloquial:

It was upside down – you know what happened, do you know how I felt? I don't remember anything. This is really the truth . . . All I remember is – I thought I fell asleep, and I was in a dream . . . I actually saw stars . . . you know, stars in the sky – y'know, when you look up there . . . and I was seein' stars. And then after a while, I felt somebody pushing and pulling – you know, they were all on top of each other – and they were pulling us out from the bottom of the car, and I was goin' 'Ooooh'. And when I came – you know – to, I says to myself, 'Ooooh, we're in a car accident,' – and that's all I remember.'[13]

But 'danger of death' memories were not the only way in which Labov elicited informal speech. He was sometimes able to overhear casual speech when the person being interviewed turned away and spoke to her children or answered the telephone. He gives a particularly interesting example of this in connection with an informant called Dolly. In the interview Dolly talked to him in a seemingly informal style, and was friendly and relaxed. For example, talking about the meaning of various words she said: 'Smart? Well, I mean, when you use the word *intelligent* an' *smart* I mean . . . you use it in the same sense? . . . (laughs). Some people are pretty witty – I mean – yet they're not so intelligent.' However, a telephone conversation which interrupted the interview showed just how different Dolly's really casual speech was: 'Huh? . . . Yeah, go down 'ere to stay. This is. So you know what Carol Ann say, "An' then when papa die, we can come back" . . . Ain't these chillun sump'm? . . . An' when papa die, can we come back?'[14]

Another woman, a thirty-five-year-old black widow with six children, was speaking about her husband who was killed in an uprising in Santo Domingo: 'I believe that those that want to go and give up their life for their country, let them go. For my part, his place was here with the children to help raise them and give them a good education... that's from my point of view.' This careful, quiet controlled style of conversation contrasted sharply with an interruption caused by one of the children: 'Get out of the refrigerator, Darlene! Tiny or Teena, or whatever your name is! . . . Close the refrigerator, Darlene! . . . What pocketbook? I don't have no pocketbook – if he lookin' for money from me, dear heart, I have no money!'[15]

Sometimes street rhymes or nursery rhymes evoked a casual style. Labov found the following one useful for his study of the vowels in *more* and *door:*

> I won't go to Macy's any more, more, more
> There's a big fat policeman at the door, door, door,
> He pulls you by the collar
> And makes you pay a dollar,
> I won't go to Macy's any more, more, more.[16]

Another way of eliciting casual speech was to allow a speaker to digress. Whenever a subject showed signs of wanting to talk, the interviewers let him go ahead. The longer he digressed, the better chance they had of studying his natural speech pattern. This worked particularly well with older speakers. Labov notes:

Some older speakers, in particular, pay little attention to the questions they are asked. They may have certain favorite points of view that they want to express, and they have a great deal of experience in making a rapid transition from the topic to the subject that is closest to their hearts.[17]

By these and similar means, Labov was able to build up a detailed picture of the fluctuating pronunciation of the sounds he examined in New York City. He found that, within the area he worked on, he could reliably predict for each ethnic group, sex, age, and social group the overall percentage of occurrence of a linguistic variable in each of four styles – casual, careful, reading prose, reading word lists. For example, he found that the upper middle class pronounced *r* in words such as *car*, *beard* just under 20 per cent of the time in casual speech, but over 30 per cent of the time in careful speech, and around 60 per cent of the time when they read word lists, whereas for the working class the comparable figures were under 10 per cent for casual speech, just over 10 per cent for careful speech, and around 30 per cent for reading word lists.[18]

Once we have a detailed and careful survey of this type, we can begin to see just how changes spread. This is the question we shall consider in the next chapter.

PART 2

Implementation

4 *Spreading the Word*

How changes spread from person to person

> You know, if one person, just one person, does it, they
> may think he's really sick . . . . And if two people do it
> . . . they may think they're both faggots. . . . And if
> three people do it! . . . . They may think it's an
> organization! . . . . And can you imagine fifty people a
> day? I said FIFTY people a day . . . . Friends, they may
> think it's a MOVEMENT, and that's what it is.
>
> Arlo Guthrie, *Alice's Restaurant*

Until recently, the origin and spread of language change
was as obscure to the majority of linguists as the sources
of disease still are to some primitive communities around
the world. The following is a typical comment by an
early-twentieth-century writer on the seemingly mysterious origins of sound change:

No records have ever been kept of these first beginnings of
regular changes of sound. . . . We know that English *wah* has
changed to *waw*, and we can give approximate dates for some
stages of this process; but we do not know when or where or in
whose pronunciation the first impulse toward the change
occurred.[1]

This statement was made over sixty years ago. It is still
true that, for the majority of past changes, we are unlikely
to know who started them, and where they began.
However, thanks to the work of scholars such as Labov,
whose methods we discussed in the last chapter, we are
now in a position to observe changes happening with far
greater accuracy than ever before. We can see how they
spread, and, in some cases, trace them to their point of
origin. This is what we shall be considering in this and the
next two chapters.

Before looking at the changes in detail, we need to distinguish between conscious and unconscious change, since this difference is likely to affect the way a change spreads. On the one hand, we find changes which people realize are happening, and actively encourage. These are triggered by 'pressures from above', that is, above the level of social awareness. On the other hand, we also find changes which people do not notice. These are influenced by 'pressures from below', that is, below the level of social awareness.[2] This is a useful preliminary distinction, even though it is not always possible to categorize changes neatly into one or the other type. In this chapter, we will look at one conscious and one unconscious one.

New York City

New Yorkers wish they did not talk like New Yorkers. Labov comments: 'In general New Yorkers show a strong dislike for the sound of New York City speech. Most have tried to change their speech in one way or another, and would be sincerely complimented to be told that they do not sound like New Yorkers.'[3] This 'sink of negative prestige'[4] is an ideal situation in which to find consciously cultivated changes, providing one can find a method of charting the apparently 'thoroughly haphazard'[5] language variation.

In the last chapter, we described how Labov tackled the problem of New York *r*. After a preliminary department-store survey, he went on to a more comprehensive analysis of *r*-usage in certain areas of New York City. Using survey techniques developed by sociologists, he obtained systematic speech samples from different socio-economic, ethnic, age and sex groups, in a variety of language styles.

Let us begin by looking at Figure 4.1 which shows some of Labov's findings.[6] The diagram below shows the per-

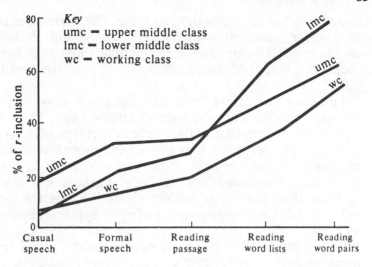

Fig. 4.1: Labov's findings on *r*-inclusion, according to class
(based on Labov, 1972)

centage of *r*-inclusion in words such as *bear, beard* in upper-middle-class (UMC), lower-middle-class (LMC) and working-class (WC) speakers for each of five speech styles: casual speech, formal speech, reading connected prose, reading word lists, and reading word pairs.

What does this chart tell us? First, it confirms the findings of the department-store survey in that it shows that *r*-insertion in words such as *bear, beard* is socially prestigious, since it occurs more frequently in the casual and formal speech of the upper middle class than in the lower social classes. A further indication of social prestige is that the more careful the speech style, the more likely *r* is to be pronounced. Obviously, when people speak slowly and carefully, they remember to insert an *r* which they feel should be there. Further evidence of its prestige value was provided by the finding that, when questioned

about whether they pronounced *r*, New Yorkers claimed
to insert *r* more often than they actually did. It is a
common observation that many people think that they
speak in a more socially prestigious way than they really
do.

The most interesting feature on the chart, however, is
the speech behaviour of the lower middle class. There is
an enormous difference between the percentage of *r*s used
in casual speech (under 10 per cent) and those inserted in
reading word lists (around 60 per cent). When they read
word lists, lower-middle-class New Yorkers use even
more *r*s than the upper middle class! What is the significance of this strange overuse of *r*, or **hypercorrection**,
as Labov calls it?

Labov claims that 'the hypercorrect behaviour of the
lower middle class is seen as a synchronic indicator of
linguistic change in progress.'[7] He suggests that members
of the lower middle class tend to be socially and linguistically insecure, and anxious to improve their low status.
More than other socio-economic classes, they are likely to
be aware of which speech forms are 'classy' prestige ones,
and will tend to insert these forms in careful speech. The
more they insert these forms in careful speech, the more
they will get into the habit of inserting *r* in casual speech.
In this way, the proportion of *r*s will gradually creep
upwards. Labov notes: 'Middle-aged, lower-middle-class
speakers tend to adopt the formal speech patterns of the
younger, upper-middle-class speakers. This tendency
provides a feed-back mechanism which is potentially
capable of accelerating the introduction of any prestige
feature.'[8] The lower-middle-class youth, he points out, will
be in contact with the new prestige pronunciation on two
fronts. On the one hand, he will be familiar with the
speech of those who are going to college, whether or not
he belongs to this group. On the other hand, his parents
and his teachers will also use this prestige pattern in
formal circumstances. He notes futhermore that hypercorrection seems to be commoner in women than in men:

'Hypercorrectness is certainly strongest in women – and it may be that the lower-middle-class mother, and the grade school teacher, are prime agents in the acceleration of this type of linguistic change.'[9]

In brief, a change 'from above' seems to be in progress in New York City, in that *r* is being increasingly inserted into words such as *beard, bear*. This change seems to be strongest in the language-conscious lower middle class, particularly lower-middle-class women, who are imitating and, in some cases, exaggerating a prestige feature found in the speech of the upper middle class.

Can we go further, and find out how *r* came to be in the speech of the upper middle class in New York in the first place? We find, on examination, that *r* has a strange, fluctuating history in American speech. We know, from spelling and other sources, that both British and American speech once had an *r* in words such as *car, card*. By the end of the eighteenth century, this *r* had disappeared from the speech of London and Boston. Then New York, apparently following the lead of these fashionable cities, lost its *r* in the next century. We have reports that it was *r*-less by the mid-nineteenth century, when for example, a New York poet rhymed *shore* with *pshaw*. It remained *r*-less in the early-twentieth century, as is confirmed by Edward Sturtevant, a linguist writing in 1917, who noted that an inserted *r* was characteristic of the western parts of the USA and likely to be a disadvantage to someone in the east: 'A strong western *r* is a distinct hindrance to a man who is trying to make his way in the East or the South of the United States.'[11] According to Sturtevant, not only was New York *r*-less, but the *r*-less pronunciation characteristic of New York was actually in the process of spreading to nearby districts: 'Another gradually spreading sound change may be observed in the neighbourhood of New York City . . . this [*r*-less] pronunciation is gradually spreading to the southwest . . . . There is little doubt that soon the whole district tributary to New York City will pronounce "caht", etc.'[12] *R*-less speech was still the norm in the 1930s, then *r* was reported to be on the increase in the 1950s and 1960s. When and how did this sudden change come about?

The re-introduction of *r*, which brought New York in line with the use of *r* in most other American dialects, seems to have occurred around the time of World War II. Labov suggests, somewhat vaguely, that 'one might argue that the experience of men in the services was somehow involved',[12] though he admits that it would be difficult to prove this suggestion. One possibility is that around this time New Yorkers had a growing awareness of themselves as American, and picked a non-British style of speech on which to model themselves. But this is speculation. All we can say is that the *r*-less pronunciation began to lose ground from the 1940s onwards.

This New York change, then, is a conscious one, in which the lower middle class are playing a prominent role. It is not altogether clear whether we are dealing with a movement towards a prestige pronunciation, or away from a stigmatized one. In another big city, Belfast, the population seems more concerned with avoiding low-prestige forms than in copying high-prestige ones.[14] This may be the case in New York also, but we cannot be sure. The change progresses as New Yorkers insert a greater proportion of *r*s in their speech, starting consciously with the most formal speech styles. We note further that *r* did not arrive 'out of the blue'. It was always present in some dialects of American English. The change occurred when these *r* dialects were taken as a prestige model by the rest of America.

New York is, in many ways, an extraordinary city. To what extent is this New York change typical of language changes in general? We will discuss this question by considering further examples of change. We will next look at a change which is rather different. It occurred on a small island, Martha's Vineyard, rather than a large city, and it took place for the most part below the level of conscious awareness.

Martha's Vineyard

One of the problems of studying sound change in a busy city like New York is that people's lives are extremely complex. Every social class, age group or ethnic group meets so many different people, and has so many conflicting influences that it is hard to know where to begin. For this reason, Labov in his early work tried to find an area which was relatively self-contained.

He chose the island known as Martha's Vineyard, which is part of the state of Massachusetts.[15] It is an island lying about three miles off the east coast of mainland America, with a permanent population of about 6000. However, this charming and picturesque island is not left undisturbed, and, much to the disgust of a number of locals, over 40,000 visitors, known somewhat disparagingly as the 'summer people' flood in every summer. More people are familiar with the appearance of Martha's Vineyard than they realize, since it was the location of the film *Jaws*. The island itself is shaped roughly like a gigantic shark, with its head lying to the east, and its tail to the west (see Figure 4.2).

The eastern part of the island is more densely populated by the permanent residents, and is the area mostly

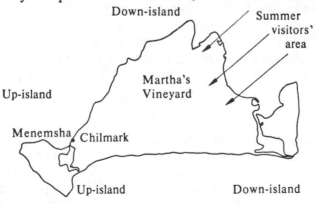

Fig. 4.2: Martha's Vineyard (based on Labov, 1972)

visited by the summer visitors, who have bought up almost the entire north-east shore, a fact deeply resented by some of the old inhabitants. As one said, 'You can cross the island from one end to the other without stepping on anything but "No Trespassing" signs.'[16] This heavily populated end of the island is generally referred to as Down-island. The western third of the island is known as Up-island. It is strictly rural, and apart from a few villages, contains salt ponds, marshes, and a large central area of uninhabited pine barrens. It is in this western part that most of the original population of the island live.

Labov made an exploratory visit to the island in order to decide which aspect of the islanders' language to study. He noted that approximately thirty years earlier, a linguist had visited Martha's Vineyard, and had at that time interviewed members of the old families of the island. When Labov compared this thirty-year-old record with his own preliminary observations, he noted that the vowel in words such as *out, trout, house*, seemed to be changing, and so, to a lesser extent, was the vowel in words such as *white, pie, night, like*. The vowel in each of these words is a diphthong, which is actually two overlapping vowels, one gliding imperceptibly into the other: [a] + [u] making [au] in the case of *house*, and [a] + [i] making [ai] in the case of *night*. In each case, the first part of the diphthong seemed to be shifting from a sound somewhat like [a] in the word *car*, towards a vowel [ə] like that at the beginning of the word *ago* or the American pronunciation of *but*:

$$[au] \rightarrow [əu]$$
$$[ai] \rightarrow [əi]$$

Labov then interviewed a cross-section of the islanders, excluding the summer visitors, after devising questions which were likely to elicit a large number of [ai] and [au] forms. For example, he asked them: 'When we speak of the *right* to *life*, liberty and the pursuit of happiness, what does *right* mean?' He also asked people to read a passage which contained further examples of the crucial sounds: 'After the *high* winds last Thursday, we went *down* to the mooring to see *how* the boat was making *out* . . . .' In this way he recorded sixty-nine formal interviews, as well as making numerous informal observations in diners, restaurants, bars, stores, and docks.

When he had obtained his results, he plotted them on a series of charts showing age, geographical distribution, ethnic group and occupation. He found that, as regards this particular change, there was no conscious awareness on the part of the islanders that it was happening. And, as a consequence of this finding, that there was no significant stylistic variation within individual speakers.

Let us now consider what he found. He discovered that the change was least in evidence in the over seventy-five year olds, and was most prominent in the thirty-one to forty-five age group. Somewhat surprisingly, the speech of the thirty and under group was less affected than that of the forty-year-olds. Geographically, the change was far more widespread in rural, western Up-island, than in the more populous Down-island. It was particularly notable in an area known as Chilmark, which formed the centre of the island's fishing activities. Once a prosperous centre of the whaling industry, Labov noted that only around 2.5 per cent of the islanders were still occupied in full-time fishing, and that this 2.5 per cent mostly lived around the Up-island village of Menemsha in Chilmark. In Down-island, on the other hand, most of the population was involved in service industries, looking after the summer visitors in various ways. When occupational groups were considered, it was the fishermen whose speech contained the highest proportion of 'local' diphthongs. The difference between ethnic groups was not so noticeable: those of English descent showed more evidence of the local pronunciation than people from Portuguese and Indian backgrounds, though not by much.

To summarize, Labov found that, compared with mainland America, a change was taking place in certain diphthongs on Martha's Vineyard. This change seemed to be most advanced in the speech of people in their thirties and early forties, and was particularly far advanced in the speech of a number of fisherman in Up-island.

Labov's survey, therefore, suggested that the change under observation possibly radiated from a small group of fishermen living in Up-island, and had then spread to people of English descent, particularly those in the thirty- to forty-five-year-old age group.

These findings raised a number of puzzling questions. First, where did the fisherman get the change from in the first place? Did one fisherman suddenly decide to alter his vowels and persuade the rest to follow him? Or what happened? Secondly, why should the adult population of Martha's Vineyard suddenly start subconsciously imitating the speech of a small and apparently insignificant bunch of fishermen?

When Labov considered these problems, he uncovered some interesting facts. He discovered that the fishermen had not suddenly altered the way they talked, as one might suppose. Instead, they had simply started to exaggerate a tendency which was already there. The 'new' diphthongs had, as far as could be ascertained, always been present to some extent in the fishermen's speech. Far from representing an innovation, the vowels in question appeared to be a conservative, old-fashioned feature in the fishermen's pronunciation, which in certain ways resembled that of mainland America in the eighteenth and nineteenth century. One of them even prided himself on preserving old values, and speaking differently from the rest of America:

You people who come down here to Martha's Vineyard don't understand the background of the old families of the island . . . strictly a maritime background and tradition . . . and what we're interested in, the rest of America, this part over here across the water that belongs to you and we don't have anything to do with, has forgotten all about . . . . I think perhaps we use entirely different . . . type of English language . . . think differently here on the island . . . it's almost a separate language within the English language.[17]

Why had the original inhabitants clung to their old speech habits, and not brought their pronunciation into line with that of the people around them? Oddly enough, there was some evidence that, some time previously, Martha's Vineyarders *had* started to lose their old diphthongs, and *had* begun to bring their vowel sounds into line with those of neighbouring mainland areas. The vowel in words such as *house*, *south* had become almost 'normal', though the vowel in *life*, *night* had lagged behind. Later, however, the almost completed change had suddenly reversed itself. The vowel in *house* had not only reverted back to its original pronunciation, but it had actually gone farther and become more extreme. This strange episode is illustrated in Figure 4.3.

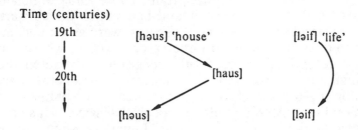

Fig. 4.3: Vowel changes on Martha's Vineyard

Why did the change which would have brought Martha's Vineyarders in line with mainland Americans suddenly reverse itself, and move in the opposite direction in an exaggerated way? And why did such a backwards move catch on among the inhabitants of the island, particularly among those of English descent between the ages of thirty and forty-five?

The answer, Labov suggests, is connected with the rise in popularity of the island as a tourist resort, and the disapproval of the summer people by the old inhabitants. The Chilmark fishermen, Labov notes, form the most close-knit social group on the island, the most independent, the one which is the most stubbornly opposed to the incursions of the summer people. The next generation down admired these old fishermen, who appeared to exemplify the virtues traditional to Martha's Vineyard: they were viewed as independent, skilful, physically strong, courageous. They epitomized the good old Yankee virtues, as opposed to the indolent consumer-oriented society of the summer visitors. This led a number of Vineyarders to sub-consciously imitate the speech characteristics of the fishermen, in order to identify themselves as 'true islanders'. This hypothesis is supported by Labov's finding that the local pronunciation was far stronger in those inhabitants who were planning to stay on the island permanently. These were mostly in the thirty- to forty-five-year age group. Those who planned to leave and live on the mainland had vowels which were more standard, and so did those who were as yet uncommitted to their future. In one case, a mother whose son had recently returned from college actually noted the change in her son, who, she suggested, was consciously adopting the speech of the fishermen. She commented: 'You know, E. didn't always speak that way . . . it's only since he came back from college. I guess he wanted to be more like the men on the docks . . . .'[18]

Let us now summarize what we have found out so far. On Martha's Vineyard a small group of fishermen began to exaggerate a tendency already existing in their speech. They did this seemingly subconsciously, in order to establish themselves as an independent social group with superior status to the despised summer visitors. A number of other islanders regarded this group as one which epitomized old virtues and desirable values, and subconsciously imitated the way its members talked. For these people, the new pronunciation was an innovation. As more and more people came to speak in the same way, the innovation gradually became the norm for those living on the island.

We may therefore divide the spread of a change such as this into a series of overlapping stages:

Stage 1 An aspect of the speech of a particular social group differs from that of the 'standard' dialect of the area. In this case, the speech of the Chilmark fishermen contained certain 'old' diphthongs which no longer existed in the standard speech of the area.

Stage 2 A second social group admires and models itself on the first group, and subconsciously adopts and exaggerates certain features in the speech of the former. In this case, Chilmark fishermen were regarded as representing traditional virtues and 'true' values by those who lived permanently on the island. The fishermen's diphthongs were subconsciously copied and exaggerated as a sign of solidarity against the despised 'summer visitors'.

Stage 3 The new speech feature gradually takes hold among those who have adopted it, and becomes the norm. In this case, the local diphthongs were adopted as the standard pronunciation by those of English descent in the thirty- to forty-five-year-old age group.

Stage 4 The process repeats itself as a new social group starts to model itself on the group which has now adopted the linguistic innovation as the norm. In this case, those of English descent in the thirty to forty-five age range were taken as models by other age groups and ethnic groups on Martha's Vineyard.

The change on Martha's Vineyard is instructive for two reasons. First, it occurred in a relatively simple social situation, where the relevant factors could be isolated without too much difficulty. Secondly, as noted above, the inhabitants of Martha's Vineyard were for the most part unaware that a change was occurring in their speech.

Superficially the New York *r* change was quite different from the one on Martha's Vineyard. Nevertheless, the changes have two notable features in common. First, they did not come 'out of the blue'. The *r* adopted by New Yorkers was always present in the speech of some if not the majority of Americans, just as the Martha's Vineyard fishermen had always retained certain 'old' vowels. Secondly, in both places the changes took hold when one group adopted another as its model. The New York *r* change occurred when New Yorkers imitated other Americans around the time of the Second World War, perhaps because of a growing awareness of themselves as being American, and requiring an American standard on which to model themselves. This *r* gradually spread among the upper middle class, who were in turn taken as a model by the socially and linguistically insecure lower middle class.

The main difference between the New York and Martha's Vineyard changes is that the New York one is above the level of conscious awareness and the Martha's Vineyard one below it. The difference may be related to how long the change has been going on. A change tends to sneak quietly into a language, like a disease which gradually infiltrates the body with minor, mostly unnoticed symptoms in the early stages. At some point in time, certain symptoms can no longer be ignored. Similarly, people may become socially aware of a change only when it reaches a certain crucial point. Another important factor, however, is the direction of the change in relation to the standard dialect of the area. Changes from above tend to be those moving in the direction of the socially accepted norm, while changes from below tend to be those moving away from it.

What happens, then, when a change from below which goes against the accepted norm suddenly becomes noticed? Does the change recede? Or does it remain in abeyance, balanced by opposing forces? These are the questions we shall be considering in the next chapter.

5 Conflicting Loyalties

Opposing social pressures within a change

> At the still point of the turning world. Neither flesh nor
> fleshless;
> Neither from nor towards; at the still point, there the
> dance is....
>
> T. S. Eliot, *Four Quartets*

In general, people do not pay much attention to the
behaviour of others, unless it is dramatically different
from the norm. A person can continue doing something
marginally odd for a long time, without calling attention
to himself. However, once people notice the oddity, they
tend to over-react. This phenomenon occurs with eating
habits, cleanliness, or personal mannerisms. People either
do not notice anything odd, or, if they do, they place the
individual concerned into a category of deviant behaviour
which probably exaggerates the situation considerably:
'Felicity drinks like a fish'; 'Marcia's house is like a
pigsty'; 'Cuthbert's continually scratching himself'.

The same thing happens with language. People either
do not notice a minor deviation from the norm, or they
over-react to it, and make comments such as 'Egbert
always drops his aitches', even though Egbert may only
drop a few of them. Consider the case of words which end
in *t* in British English, such as *what, hot*. A very large
number of people alter *t* to a glottal stop when it occurs
before another word, as in *wha(t) stupidity, ho(t) water
bottle*, but they usually do not realize they are doing so,
nor do they notice other people doing so. Others, however, also change *t* at the end of a sentence, as in
Wha(t)? It's ho(t). This is usually noticed, and often
censured. We frequently hear parents upbraiding their
children with comments such as, 'Don'(t) say "*wha(t)*" in

tha(t) sloppy way!', not realizing that their own speech shows a fluctuating *t* also. *T*-dropping, then, is a change against the standard norm which has emerged into public view when it occurs in certain linguistic environments. Similarly, in the city of Norwich the standard British English forms *walking, talking* alternate with forms ending in *n*: *walkin', talkin'*. Labov notes that listeners react in one of two ways to these *walkin' talkin'* forms: 'Up to a certain point they do not perceive the speaker "dropping his *g*'s" at all; beyond a certain point, they perceive him as always doing so.'[1] At both times, there is likely in fact to have been fluctuation, but this fluctuation is not perceived by the listener.

Let us now consider what happens when a non-standard linguistic feature suddenly emerges into popular consciousness. This can happen either when a change from below becomes noticed, or when a dialect feature which has existed in the language for some time is perceived as clashing with a spreading standard feature. In both cases there will be conflict between the social forces which fostered the non-standard feature, and those promoting the accepted norm. At this point, one sometimes finds a period of apparent calm – the change superficially stops. On closer examination, however, we see that it is the artificial calm in the centre of the cyclone, a momentary balance of opposing social factors. As in the Eliot quotation above, 'at the still point, there the dance is'. Let us go on to examine this type of situation. We will look at the case mentioned above of *g*-dropping in Norwich.

Walkin' and talkin' in Norwich

> The man in the moon
> Came down too soon
> And asked his way to Norwich;
> He went by the south
> And burnt his mouth
> With supping cold plum porridge.[2]

If the man in the moon came down today, he probably wouldn't want to go to Norwich, a smallish city in East Anglia, situated a few miles from the east coast of England. The children's rhyme quoted above is perhaps a memory from the sixteenth and seventeenth centuries when Norwich briefly laid claim to being the second largest city in England. Nowadays, however, it is small in comparison with big cities such as London or Birmingham, though it remains a centre of considerable cultural and commercial importance for the surrounding area. Communications with the rest of England are not good, and according to one facetious account it is 'cut off on three sides by the sea and the fourth by British Rail'.[3]

The relatively cut-off situation of Norwich suggested that it might be an interesting area in which to study language change. Standard British English, spreading from London, was likely to interact in interesting ways with local speech habits which remain entrenched because of the traditional independence and relative isolation of the area. And so it proved.

Norwich speech was studied by Peter Trudgill, a one-time native of the city,[4] now at the University of Reading. Using Labov-type methods, he interviewed a cross-section of the population, eliciting the same four speech styles as Labov: casual speech, formal speech, reading passages and word lists. He confirmed Labov's finding that, when there is both class and stylistic variation, a change is likely to be in progress. More interesting than the actual changes he charted, however, was one which seemed to be in the balance, held in abeyance by opposing forces, like a car driver who has his foot pressed partially on the clutch and partially on the accelerator, so the car remains motionless in the middle of a hill, running neither forwards nor backwards. Trudgill found a situation like this when he examined the final consonant in words such as *walking, running*. In standard British English, the sound spelled -*ng* is a so-called 'velar nasal' [ŋ]. In Norwich, however, the pronunciation *walkin'*, *talkin'* is frequently heard, as if there was simply *n* on the end. This is a remnant of an older style of speech. The ending *-in'* for *talkin'*, *walkin'*, used to be considerably more common, and even in the 1930s was an acceptable pronunciation among large sections of speakers of standard British English. Its widespread usage in the past is shown in rhymes and misspellings. For example, Shakespeare's *cushing*, *javeling* for 'cushion', 'javelin', which were never pronounced with *-ing*, indicate that he added *g* because he thought it ought to be there in the spelling. More vividly, consider Swift's couplet (dating from around 1700) in which *fitting* and *spit in* rhyme:

> His jordan [=chamber pot] stood in manner fitting
> Between his legs, to spew or spit in.[5]

The currently standard use of the *-ing* (velar nasal) pronunciation was perhaps due to the spread of a hypercorrect pronunciation in the first part of the nineteenth century, an imposed pattern like New York *r*. In Norwich, this pattern was never fully imposed, and local *-in'* remained. Recently, however, the alternation between local *-in'* and standard British *-ing* has emerged into speakers' consciousness, resulting in a conflict of great interest to anyone interested in the mechanisms of linguistic change. Trudgill noted an interplay not only between social classes, but also, as in the New York change, between the sexes.

At first, Trudgill's results did not look particularly surprising. He found that in all social classes, the more careful the speech, the more likely people were to say *walking* rather than *walkin'*. *Walkin'* was definitely a feature of casual, not careful speech. He also found that the proportion of *walkin'*-type forms was higher in the lower social classes. Forms such as *walkin'*, *talkin'*, appeared 100 per cent of the time in the casual speech of the lower working class, for example, but only 28 per cent of the time in the casual speech of the middle middle class. This is entirely the result that one might have expected. But when he examined his results more carefully, he found an interesting phenomenon. The nonstandard forms occurred considerably more often in men's speech than in women's in *all* social classes. This is illustrated in Figure 5.1[6] below which compares the percentage of *walkin'*-type forms in the speech of middle-middle-class and lower-working-class men and women.

Judging by these figures, there appears to be a tug-of-war going on, with the men pulling one way, and the women the other. The men are pulling away from the overt prestige form, and the women are pulling toward it. This was further confirmed when Trudgill questioned people from both sexes about what they thought they were saying. He found that women thought they were using the standard form more often than they in fact were, whereas men tended to give the opposite response. They claimed to be using the *non*-standard form more often

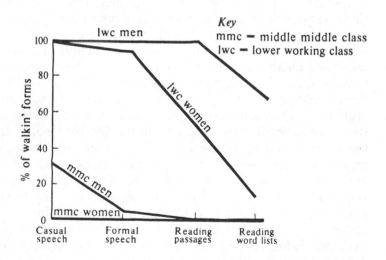

Fig. 5.1: Walkin' and talkin' in Norwich (based on Trudgill, 1974)

than they actually were! This reflects wishful thinking in both cases. The women wanted to think of themselves as speaking the standard prestige form, whereas the men wanted to think of themselves as speaking the 'rougher' speech of their fellow workers.

Trudgill suggests two related reasons for this phenomenon.[7] First, women in our society are more status-conscious than men, and are therefore more aware of the social significance of different speech forms. Secondly, male working-class speech tends to be associated with roughness and toughness, which are considered by many to be desirable masculine attributes, though not desirable feminine ones. He goes on to suggest that conscious changes may well be initiated by women. Women are consciously striving to 'speak better', partly because of a certain social insecurity, partly because they are not aiming to sound 'tough'. They presumably encourage their children to talk in a socially acceptable way, and so aid changes in the direction of the standard language. Subconscious changes, on the other hand, may well be initiated by working-class men. Other men tend to admire their supposed masculinity and toughness and imitate them, often without realizing they are doing so. These suggestions are supported by the New York and Martha's Vineyard changes. In New York, *r*-insertion was led by lower-middle-class women. On Martha's Vineyard, the vowel change was initiated by a group of fishermen. In fact, this difference between the sexes appears to be a widespread phenomenon, at least in the Western world. It has been found in Switzerland, Paris, Detroit, Chicago and New York, and most people can provide anecdotal evidence to support it in other areas also. We all know couples like Edna and Eric who were of working-class Liverpool stock, but who came south and moved into the fashionable 'stockbroker belt' on the outer fringes of London. Edna rapidly lost her working-class Liverpool accent, though Eric retained his for the rest of his life.

To return to *walkin'*, *talkin'*, we cannot predict a movement in any one direction, as there seems to be a pull between the *walkin'* pronunciation, which has covert prestige, and the *walking* pronunciation with overt prestige. It will be interesting to see which one wins out in the future. Overall, the tug-of-war provides a useful guide to social pressures within a community, and the progress or regression of a change reflects this changing struggle.

Note that all the changes we have considered so far have been sound changes. Let us now go on to look at a syntactic change – change in the form and arrangement of words – which is in certain respects like the Norwich change just considered, in that it again represents a conflict between opposing social pressures.

We knows how to talk in Reading

'Syntactic change', Labov notes, 'is an elusive process as compared to sound change; whereas we find sound changes in progress in every large city in the English-speaking world, we have comparatively little data on syntactic change.'[8] Part of the trickiness and mystery of syntactic change may be because the changes tend to occur very slowly, slower in general than sound changes. This makes it less easy to chart their origin and growth. Another reason why syntactic change seems so elusive is undoubtedly because relatively few people have studied it in any depth. Several decades ago, as we saw, sound change was considered to be a mystical and unobservable wraith. Now it is syntactic change which is causing puzzlement. We are beginning to understand it, however, as an increasing number of people (including Labov himself) develop Labov-type techniques for working on it.

Here, we shall consider one recent, detailed study which sheds considerable light on the question of changing verb forms in Reading, England, carried out by Jenny

Cheshire, a linguist at the University of Bath.[9] In Reading, it is not uncommon to hear sentences such as:

I *knows* how to handle teddy boys
You *knows* my sister, the one who's small
They *calls* me all the names under the sun

where standard British English would use *I know, you know, they call*. Cheshire studied the incidence of these non-standard verb forms in the speech of a number of adolescents in adventure playgrounds. These playgrounds were all seen as 'trouble spots' by the local residents because of the fights and fires that took place there, and the children concerned were in many cases 'tough' children who swore, fought, uttered obscenities and did not go to school regularly. In all, twenty-five children were studied: thirteen boys and twelve girls. Their ages ranged from nine to seventeen, though most were between eleven and fifteen. They were loosely clustered into three groups, two of boys and one of girls.

Superficially, the use of these non-standard verbs alternated randomly with the use of the conventional forms in the speech of these adolescents. Careful analysis, however, showed that there was a clear pattern in their distribution. In casual speech, the overall average of the non-standard forms was fairly high, around 55 per cent. In formal speech, when the children were recorded in the presence of their schoolteacher, the percentage dropped to less than half this total, around 25 per cent. The girls seemed more aware of the need to conform to standard English in a formal situation than the boys. There was relatively little difference between the sexes in the number of non-standard forms in casual speech, but in formal speech the percentage of non-standard forms was much lower in the girls than the boys: the girls adjusted their speech more sharply in the direction of 'acceptable' English than the boys did. This is shown in the table below which shows the percentage of non-standard forms

in the casual and formal speech of the three groups
studied:

	Casual (%)	Formal (%)
Boys (1)	54	27
(2)	66	35
Girls	49	13

We noticed in our discussion of sound change that
women tend towards the standard 'prestige' pronunciation. The figures above suggest that this works for syntax
also. Further light was shed on this phenomenon when
Cheshire analysed the individual speech of each child – an
analysis which showed, however, that sex was not the only
relevant social factor. More crucial was the extent to
which the individual concerned conformed to the de-
mands of the local adolescent sub-culture which required
a youngster to be 'tough'. The use of non-standard verb
forms was closely correlated with 'toughness'.

Consider Noddy, the boy who used non-standard forms
most often – around 81 per cent of the time. Noddy, the
investigator discovered, was one of the 'central core'
members of the first boys' group. He scored high on a
'toughness' index, in that he figured in stories about past
fights, was reputed to be a good fighter, carried a weapon,
took part in shoplifting or in setting fire to buildings, and
did not lose his nerve when confronted by a policeman. In
addition, Noddy scored high on an 'ambition to do a
tough job' index. He wanted to be a slaughterer like his
father rather than a teacher or someone who worked in an
office or shop. Noddy, then, was seen as a 'tough' central
member of his group, and enjoyed considerable social
prestige among his contemporaries. The other two boys
who had a high percentage of non-standard verb forms in
their speech, Perry and Ricky, also had high status among
their contemporaries, for the same reasons as Noddy.

Let us compare Noddy with Kevin, a boy who used
non-standard forms only 14 per cent of the time. Kevin

was not really part of the group at all. He was only around so much because he lived in the pub next door to the playground where the group met. He was often jeered at and excluded from group activities by the other boys, but seemed to have decided that the best way of getting along with them was to allow himself to be the butt of the group's jokes. His toughness rating was low, and he wanted to do a white-collar job.

It seems, then, that the use of non-standard verb forms among the boys was closely correlated with toughness and 'core' membership of a group. What about the girls? The girls did not go in for toughness like the boys. Their interests were generally pop singers and boyfriends. They disliked school, often stayed away, and looked forward to the time when they could leave and, hopefully, get married and have children. Four girls however, Dawn, Margaret, Karen and Linda, stood out from the others in that they attended school regularly, did not swear or steal, and said that the other girls were 'rough' or common. These girls had a far lower percentage of non-standard verb forms in their casual speech, around 26 per cent compared with the 58 per cent which was the average for the rest of the girls.

This pattern of non-standard forms favoured by 'tough' boys, and standard forms used by 'goody-goody' girls strikes a familiar note. The pull between *I knows* and *I know* in Reading seems to be surprisingly similar to the pull between *walkin'* and *walking* in Norwich. In both cases, the non-standard forms are preferred by males and have covert prestige, whereas the standard forms are favoured by females and have overt prestige, resulting in a tug-of-war situation.

Where did the Reading boys get forms such as *I knows*, *you knows* from? Did they make them up to be different? No one knows the answer for sure, but there is some evidence that these forms are not an innovation, but a relic from an earlier time when, in south-western dialects of English, there was an -s all the way through the present tense: *I knows, you knows, he knows, we knows, they knows*. This verbal paradigm gradually lost ground as standard British English spread from London. So it is likely that the Reading adolescents are not innovators, but are maintaining an old tradition, and in so doing are delaying a change which may be spreading from above towards standard British English.

Summary

Let us now summarize the contents of the last two chapters. We have looked at how changes spread from person to person, where they are likely to start, and the circumstances under which they are likely to take hold. We have noted first that changes are not, for the most part, comparable to meteorites falling from the sky. They usually originate from elements already in the language which get borrowed and exaggerated, just as changes in fashion in clothes are usually borrowings and adaptations from, say, the apparel of Moroccan peasants, rather than inventions in a vacuum.

Secondly, we noted that there is a grain of truth in the popular notion that changes are catching, like a disease, since people tend to conform to the speech habits of those around them. In other respects, however, the disease metaphor breaks down. People do not want to catch a disease. They do, however, want to talk like those they are imitating, even if they are not aware of it. A change occurs when one group consciously or subconsciously takes another as its model, and copies features from its speech. The situation is somewhat like that described in Robert Browning's poem, 'The Lost Leader':

We that had loved him so, followed him, honoured him,
Lived in his mild and magnificent eye,
Learned his great language, caught his clear accents,
Made him our pattern to live and to die!

Thirdly, we noted that conscious changes are usually in the direction of speech forms with overt prestige, such as standard British English, and that these often originate with the upper working class, or lower middle class, particularly women from these classes. Subconscious changes are often movements away from overt prestige forms, and often begin with working-class men, whose speech and habits are associated with toughness and virility, and so have covert prestige.

Typically changes spread, though this is not inevitable. When a subconscious change which has been going on for some time reaches the level of social awareness, or when an old well-established feature is observed to clash with a newer standard form, there is sometimes a tug-of-war between the old and the new which may go on for decades, or even centuries.

The spread of language change, then, is essentially a social phenomenon, which reflects the changing social situation. Changes do not occur unless they have some type of prestige. They are markers of group membership, and people outside the group want, consciously or subconsciously, to belong. It would, however, be a mistake to assume that social factors alone are all we need to know about. Let us now go on to look at some strictly linguistic matters by considering another facet of language change, its spread through the language concerned.

6 Catching on and Taking off

How changes spread through a language

Large streams from little fountains flow,
Tall oaks from little acorns grow.
David Everett, *Lines Written for a School Declamation*

So far, we have looked only at the sociolinguistic aspects of language change – how a change spreads through a community. We now need to look at the linguistic aspects – how a change spreads through a language. Just as with a disease we need to know what was the first symptom, and how it spread through the body, so in language change we need to know where a change starts and how it diffuses through a language. In the words of Edward Sapir, a sound change is a 'consummated drift that sets in at a psychologically exposed point and worms its way through a gamut of psychologically analogous forms'.[1] We need to know what is meant by 'a psychologically exposed point', and just how a change 'worms its way through'.

Until relatively recently, this was a question neglected by the majority of linguists, who did not realize that anything needed explaining. It was widely assumed that a sound change affected all the relevant words in a dialect simultaneously. This belief dated back to the so-called Neogrammarians, a group of scholars centred on Leipzig around 1870. In the words of two of the most famous, 'All sound changes, as mechanical processes, take place according to laws with no exceptions'[2] – implying that sound changes were controlled, as it were, by a master switch which altered the sound in question to the same extent in all the words concerned, automatically and simultaneously. This strange assumption was based on the belief that sound changes were purely a matter of physiology, beyond the conscious awareness of the speaker. 'The regularity in the transmission of sounds results from changes in the articulatory system and not the articulation of an isolated word', said one famous French linguist at the end of the last century.[3]

Yet when linguists started actually looking at changes instead of simply theorizing about them, they found that this supposed mechanical simultaneity just did not exist. Instead, the change affected different words at different times – as is clear from even a cursory glance at New York's fluctuating *r*.

The question then arises: which words were affected? Was there some consistent pattern? When Labov examined this question, he noticed that some words tended to get affected before others, but even those most affected did not receive the 'new' pronunciation every time. Speakers used different forms of the same word on different days, and, on more than one occasion, different forms of the same word in a single sentence. For example, on one day a New Yorker read the sentence 'He darted out about four feet before a car, and he got hit hard', inserting an *r* into *darted*, *car*, and *hard*. The next time she read it, some days later, she missed out the *r* in *hard*.[4] Similarly, a Martha's Vineyard fisherman used the word *knife* twice within the same sentence, once with a local vowel, and once with a fairly standard one.[5]

It would, however, be a mistake to think that the situation was one of pure chaos. In the start and progress of a change, certain consistent factors are beginning to emerge. We can, with some degree of confidence, build up a profile of a 'typical' change. This is what we shall do in the current chapter.

Getting a foothold

Trying to find out where a change started is like trying to locate the epicentre of an earthquake some years after the event. Our best chance of discovering some general facts about how changes begin, therefore, is to look at changes in progress. We can note which words have been affected, and try to find the reason.

There is a growing body of evidence that frequently used words quite often get affected early – an observation first made in the nineteenth century. As examples, let us look at two changes in English which have started with such words, but have not yet progressed to infrequently used ones. These changes are happening independently in certain varieties of British, American and Australian English.

Consider the words *adultery, century, cursory, delivery, desultory, elementary, every, factory, nursery, slavery*. If possible, write them down on a piece of paper and ask several friends to read them out loud. Better still, get people to read sentences which include the words such as, 'A *cursory* glance at the newspapers suggests that *adultery* is on the increase in this *century*'. 'If you think *slavery* has been abolished, go and look at the *factory* at the end of our road'. '*Every* mother will tell you that *nursery* schools are a mixed blessing'. Make a careful note of how the crucial words are pronounced, and see if your results agree with those of a linguist who recently carried out an investigation of this type.[6]

The investigator noted that, according to the dictionary, all words which are spelt with *-ary, -ery, -ory*, or *-ury*, are pronounced somewhat as if they rhymed with *furry*. The vowel preceding *r* is a so-called **schwa**, a short indeterminate sound written phonetically as [ə], and sometimes represented orthographically as *er* (British English) or *uh* (American English). In practice, the schwa was not always pronounced. It was usually omitted in common words such a *ev(e)ry, fact(o)ry, nurs(e)ry*, which were pronounced as if they were spelled *evry, factry, nursry* with two syllables only. In slightly less common words, such as *delivery*, there was fluctuation. Some people inserted a schwa, others omitted it. A schwa was

retained in the least common words, such as *desultory,
cursory.*

A similar thing is happening in another set of words,
those with an unstressed first syllable.[7] Say the names of
the months through to yourself, at normal conversational
speed. The last four, *September, October, November,
December,* all have an unstressed first syllable, If an
unstressed first syllable is followed by a single consonant,
it is common for the vowel to be reduced to schwa, as in
November, December. But if the unstressed vowel is
followed by two consonants, as in *September, October,*
the full original vowel normally remains. This has been
the situation for some time. Recently, however, schwa
has started to creep into the first syllable of common
words when two consonants follow. In conversation, the
words *mistake, astronomy, mosquito, despair,* quite often
have schwa in their first syllable, whereas less common
words with a similar structure, such as *mistook, esquire*
and *muscology,* retain a fuller vowel. This phenomenon can
also be observed intermittently in the conversation of people
talking about places, objects and activities which they refer
to often. For instance, Australians reduce the first vowel in
the word *Australia,* while the rest of the world tends to use
the full vowel. New Yorkers reduce the first vowel in *Manhattan,* and professional trombonists do the same with the
first vowel in *trombone.*

Interacting with frequency of use is another factor
which is often indistinguishable from it, that of the
importance of a word within a particular subculture. This
is illustrated by the Reading adolescents discussed in the
last chapter. They show that language features which
characterize a particular subculture, such as their non-
standard verb endings, tend to get attached to words
which typify that culture.[8] The Reading teenagers had a
number of 'special' verbs, verbs which are either not used
in standard English, or are used with a different meaning,
as in 'We fucking chins them with bottles' (with *chin*
meaning 'hit on the chin'); 'We bunks it over here a lot'

(with *bunk* meaning 'play truant'); 'we kills them' (with *kill* meaning 'beat in a fight'); 'I legs it up Blagdon Hill' (with *leg it* meaning 'run away'). The non-standard *-s* ending was attached to these verbs over 90 per cent of the time in all three groups of teenagers studied, whereas the non-standard *-s* was attached to other verbs merely around 50 per cent of the time. The fact that language features which characterize a particular group are often associated with words special to that group may have one of two consequences. On the one hand, it can enable a change to get a foothold. On the other hand, it can (as in the case of the Reading teenagers) retard a movement towards the norm.

The effect of both frequency and cultural importance is detectable in a change happening in certain Dravidian languages, a group of languages spoken mainly in southern India and Ceylon.[9] This particular change is progressing exceptionally slowly. It has been going on now for around two millennia, and is apparently still in progress. In it, *r* in the middle of words is gradually making its way to the front. For example, **ūz-* 'to plough' became *ūr-* then *rū-*. Because the change is moving so slowly, it has been possible to discover from past records which words were affected first. They turn out to be words fundamental to the culture, such as *two, moon, month, burn, open, enter*, which are also presumably relatively frequent ones.

Note, however, that frequency or importance in a culture are not the only factors to be taken into consideration. Words can only be in the forefront of a change if they are linguistically susceptible to that particular change. In every change, there are likely to be factors which are outside the conscious control of the speakers. This is illustrated at its simplest by the loss of schwa in words such as *fam(i)ly, ev(e)ry*. The words in the vanguard of this particular change are not only frequent ones, but also those in which the resulting new sequence of consonants is easy to pronounce. The change has not affected common words such as *burglary*, *forgery*, where the resulting new sequence would be the unusual and difficult to pronounce combinations [glr] and [dʒr].

A less obvious example of linguistic susceptibility occurred in the Martha's Vineyard changes where words beginning with a vowel tended to be the most affected, so that *I* was more susceptible than *my*, and *out* more than *trout*. Similarly, words ending in *t* tended to be more involved than those ending in *d* or *n*, so *right* and *night* were more affected than *side* and *tide*, and *out* and *trout* more than *down* and *round*.[10]

In the Reading situation also, there were linguistic factors beyond the teenagers' control. Without realizing it, the adolescents invariably used standard forms such as *I know*, *I believe*, *I think*, in certain types of complex sentence – sentences which contain more than one verb.[11] If, in a sentence with a main verb and a subordinate verb, the subordinate verb had an ending -*s*, then the teenagers always omitted the -*s* from the main verb. So we find sentences such as:

I believe that there is, you know, life after death
You know if anything breaks on that pushchair . . .

instead of *I believes* or *you knows*. It is noticeable that this phenomenon occurred even in the speech of Noddy who, as we have seen, used non-standard verb forms most of the time. This is an interesting example of how unconscious linguistic factors are at work in language all the time, either helping changes to gain a foothold, or retarding them and preventing them from 'taking off'.

Changes then, often start in words that are frequent, and/or in those that typify a particular subculture, provided that they are linguistically susceptible to the particular change. Note that although such words *may* be in the vanguard of a change, they are not invariably so. They may, in other circumstances, retard or even be left out of changes, as in the case of the verb *to be* which is irregular and archaic in form in many of the world's languages. In short, 'frequent words can do exceptional things'.[12]

Once a change has got a firm foothold in certain words, it will probably catch on and spread to others. Let us now look at this process of 'catching on'.

Catching on

Once a change has gained a foothold in a few common words, or group of words important to a particular subculture, it is likely to start moving through the vocabulary. This is a messy business, with different words affected at different times. Amidst general fluctuation, change spreads gradually across the lexicon (vocabulary) of the language, one or two words at a time. This word-by-word progress is known as **lexical diffusion**.[13]

A Welsh change is particularly instructive.[14] Words beginning with *chw-* . . . , such as *chwaer* 'sister', *chwannen* 'flea', were at one time pronounced with a soft *khw*-like sound [xw] at the beginning. Then this initial consonant began to disappear, first in South Wales, then in Central Wales, and finally in the north. When the progress of this change was examined, an interesting phenomenon emerged. Even when the initial sequence *chw-* was followed by the same vowel, different words lost their initial consonant at different times. Take the three words *chwarae* 'to play', *chwannen* 'flea', and *chwaer* 'sister' in Figure 6.1. One of these three words was likely to lose its initial consonant without there being any alteration in the other two at first. Then the change was likely to affect one of the remaining two, then all three.

Lexical diffusion can also be seen in a slow-moving change that is creeping through English, affecting the stress pattern of certain nouns with two syllables.[15] Read out loud the sentence, 'He hid the treasure in a recess in the wall', and ask other people to do so too. Where did you and your informants place the stress on the word

Fig. 6.1: Consonant loss in three Welsh words

recess? According to the 1976 edition of the *Concise Oxford Dictionary*, it should be accented on the last syllable, *recéss*. But many people in England and almost everybody in America now place the stress on the first syllable, *récess*. The history of this ongoing change goes back four centuries or so. In the early-sixteenth century, there were a number of two-syllable words which could be either a verb or noun. All of these were stressed on the second syllable. The stress shift began, apparently, in the second half of the sixteenth century. By 1570, according to a dictionary published at the time, three words, *outlaw*, *rebel* and *record* had moved the stress on the noun to the first syllable, giving pairs such as *récord*, noun, as in 'We keep a *récord* of Fergus's cute little sayings' and *recórd*, verb, as in 'We *recórd* Fergus's cute little sayings'. Twelve years later, in 1582, another five items had been added. There were 24 by 1660, 35 by 1700, 70 by 1800, and 150 by 1934, according to one count. This gradual climb through the vocabulary is illustrated in Figure 6.2. In spite of the seemingly large number of words affected, such as *áddict*, *áffix*, *cónvict*, *défect*, there are still around a thousand which the change has not yet reached, such as *mistáke*, *dislíke*, *repórt*. One that is wavering at the current time is *address*, as in 'What's your *address*?' Some people, particularly Americans, say *áddress*, others still prefer *addréss*. Since the change seems to be working its way through the

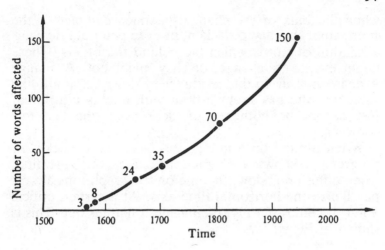

Fig. 6.2: Stress shift in nouns such as *Convict*

language, it is likely that *áddress* will become the standard form, and that other words, as yet unaffected, will begin to waver.

Taking off

Can we say anything more about the way a change diffuses? One obvious question involves the rate of diffusion. Does a change proceed through a language at a steady pace, like a tortoise climbing up a hill? Or does it leap forward by fits and starts? Or is there any other discernible pattern? Recent research suggests that a typical change fits into a slow-quick-quick-slow pattern.

In the majority of cases, an innovation starts slowly, affecting relatively few words. When a certain number has been affected, the innovation gathers momentum. There comes a sudden 'take off' point when a great number of words are affected in a relatively short time span. Then, when the bulk of the change has been completed, the momentum appears to slacken, or even peter out, leaving a handful of words which lag behind the others. These might eventually change, or they might not. A change appears to clear up this residue very slowly, if at all, like someone who has swept a floor with mighty effort, but just cannot be bothered to clear away the last few cobwebs.

When plotted on a graph, this slow-quick-quick-slow progression shows a characteristic S-curve.[16] At first, when diffusion is slow, the line on the graph runs almost parallel to the horizontal time axis. At a certain critical point, it climbs sharply, then again it flattens out. This is shown in Figure 6.3.

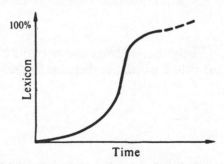

Fig. 6.3: S-curve progression of sound change (based on Chen, 1972)

An example of a change which is virtually complete, and so shows a characteristic S-curve, is found in spoken French, in the loss of final [n] in words such as *an* 'year', *en* 'in', *fin* 'end', *bon* 'good', *brun* 'brown'.[17] Starting in the tenth century, this final [n] was lost, and the preceding vowel nasalized (pronounced with the air expelled partially through the nose). This is demonstrated in Figure 6.4.

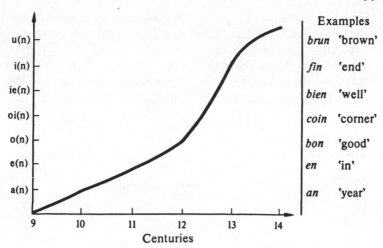

Examples

u(n)	*brun*	'brown'
i(n)	*fin*	'end'
ie(n)	*bien*	'well'
oi(n)	*coin*	'corner'
o(n)	*bon*	'good'
e(n)	*en*	'in'
a(n)	*an*	'year'

Centuries

Fig. 6.4: Change in French words ending in – *n*

As can be seen, this change started relatively slowly in the tenth and eleventh centuries. It speeded up in the twelfth and thirteenth, then slowed down again in the fourteenth.

Overlapping S-curves

The slow-quick-quick-slow pattern of an S-curve is found in a large number of changes. A closer look at each S-curve, however, suggests that many S-curves are themselves composed of smaller S-curves. Each little S-curve covers one particular linguistic environment. Take the loss of final *n* in French, an S-curve which stretched over five centuries or so. It seems likely that each separate vowel had a smaller S-curve within the big S-curve. So the loss of *n* after *a*, as in *an* 'year', itself occurred as a little

S-curve. The change spread to a few examples of *-an*, then to the majority, then finally rounded up the few remaining stragglers. After this it proceeded to *-en*, following the same procedure. However, the stragglers in *-an* overlapped with the earliest *-en* changes, so, in effect we have a series of overlapping S-curves, as in Figure 6.5.

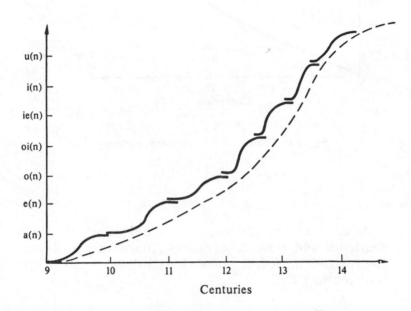

Fig. 6.5: Overlapping S-curves (French words in *-n*)

A series of overlapping S-curves actually in progress has been found recently in the Shuang-feng dialect of Chinese.[18] In this dialect, a change is in progress altering voiced stops at the beginning of words into voiceless ones.

(A **voiced stop** is one whose production involves the vibration of the vocal cords as in [b], [d], [g], as opposed to **voiceless stops** such as [p], [t], [k], in which the vocal cords do not vibrate. This vibration can be felt by placing a finger on one's Adam's apple while the sound is being uttered). Chinese, unlike English, distinguishes between words not only by means of contrast between the actual sounds, but also on the basis of tone or pitch of the voice. This particular change seems to be moving from tone to tone, starting with tone IV in a series of overlapping S-curves. The exact situation is shown below.

Tone	Number of words	Voiced (unchanged)	Voiceless (changed)	Changed (%)
IV	88	4	84	94.5
III	140	120	20	16.67
II	100	90	10	10
I	288	286	2	0.7

These figures can be interpreted as follows: a change is in progress altering voiced stops at the beginning of words into voiceless ones. This change reached tone IV words first. Here 95.45 per cent of possible words already have the new pronunciation, so the change is almost complete for this tone. The S-curve has flattened off, and there is a four-word residue which may be dealt with at some future time. The change has started on tone III, and with 16.67 per cent of words affected, has perhaps reached take-off point. Tone II is following relatively closely behind tone III, showing that the overall curve is steepening. Tone 1 is virtually unaffected, with only two altered words. The situation is shown in Figure 6.6.

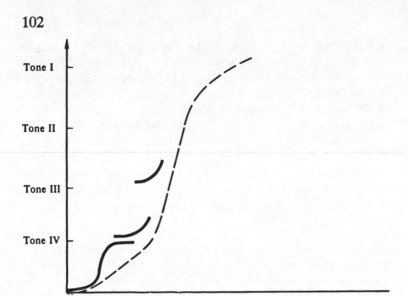

Fig. 6.6: Early stages of an S-curve (Shuang-feng dialect of Chinese)

The tendency of a change to spread from one linguistic environment to another is sometimes referred to by linguists as **rule generalization**, a name which is self-explanatory, since a particular linguistic rule becomes generalized to an ever wider range of environments. Rule generalization can sometimes be deceptive, since later generations may misinterpret a series of overlapping events as one single sweeping catastrophe. Many people, for example, assume that in French there was a sudden and sweeping loss of final *n*, when in fact there was a series of overlapping events which occurred over the course of centuries.

Syntactic change

So far in this chapter, we have talked only about sound change. But syntactic change seems to spread in a very similar way. This is evident in the history of English modal verbs, verbs such as *can, may, shall, must, will.*[19] Today, they behave rather differently from ordinary verbs, as can be seen from the chart below, which indicates some of the major differences between a modal such as *will* and an ordinary verb such as *washed*. (An asterisk signifies an impossible sentence):

	Modal	Ordinary verb
Direct object	*Alice must the cat	Alice washed the cat
to + verb	*To must the cat was stupid	To wash the cat was stupid
Verb + *-ing*	*Musting the cat was stupid	Washing the cat was stupid
Inversion	Must Alice try again?	*Tries Alice again?
Modal + *not*	Alice must not try again	*Alice tries not again

Originally, none of these differences existed. Modals could occur with direct objects, as in *Yet can I musick too* 'Yet I can make music too', after *to*, as in *to may*, and with an *-ing* suffix, as in *maeyinge*. Meanwhile, ordinary verbs could undergo inversion and be followed by the negative *not*, as shown by a number of lines of Shakespeare: 'Thinkst thou I'd make a life of jealousy?'[20] 'You go not, till I set you up a glass . . . .'[21]

The separation of modals from other verbs happened gradually. First, they stopped taking direct objects. Then in the sixteenth century came a bunch of changes. They no longer occurred with *-ing* or after *to*, they were no longer found with *have*, and they were limited to one per sentence. In the seventeenth century, ordinary verbs stopped undergoing inversion, and no longer preceded the negative *not*. In brief, we seem to have a syntactic S-curve, with the steep part of the curve occurring in the sixteenth century.

Another change which seems to be following an S-curve pattern in present–day English involves the so-called 'progressive'.[22] This construction consists of part of the verb *to be* followed by a verb ending in *-ing*, as in *Tom is having a bath*, or *Felix is drinking whisky*. It is called the 'progressive' because it is, or was, mainly used to indicate that an action was currently in progress, as in the examples above, which suggest that Tom is actually in the process of having a bath, and Felix is halfway through a glass of whisky.

The construction started slowly. Occasional progressive forms are found in the English of 1000 years ago, in the heroic epic *Beowulf*, and in King Alfred's translations from Latin. It occurs from time to time in Shakespeare. For example, at one point Antony says, 'I am dying, Egypt, dying',[23] though a little earlier he had said, 'I come, my queen',[24] when it would sound considerably more natural to us to say, 'I'm coming'. Since then, there has been a gradual increase in the use of the progressive. It is now the normal form for an ongoing action. Anyone who said 'What do you read, my lord?' as Polonius did to Hamlet,[25] instead of 'What are you reading?' would be considered very odd. In addition, the progressive has now spread beyond its original use of indicating an action in progress. Increasingly, we hear people saying things like: *Tom is having a bath as soon as Arabella is out of the bathroom*, or *Felix is tired of whisky, he's drinking gin these days*, when at the time of the conversation, Tom is possibly washing his car, and Felix cleaning his teeth.

Furthermore, there used to be a set of verbs expressing mental states which were never normally used with the progressive, even when they indicated an action in progress as in:

Ursula loves God (not *Ursula is loving God).
Angela knows my brother (not *Angela is knowing my brother).
I understand French (not *I am understanding French).

Nowadays, however, one hears an increasing number of sentences in which mental state verbs are found with the progessive:

Billy is kissing Petronella, and *is loving* it.
The matron does not know all she should *be knowing* about this affair.[26]
Charles *is understanding* French a lot better since he's been to France.

A related change is the sudden expansion of *going to*, to express the future. This construction occurred occasionally in Shakespeare, usually when someone was literally on his way to do something, as in 'I am going to visit the prisoner',[27] meaning 'I am on my way to visit the prisoner'. In Dickens' novel *Oliver Twist*, written in the mid-nineteenth century, it occurs twenty-four times and accounts for 4 per cent of expressions of future time. In Salinger's *Catcher in the Rye*, written in the mid-twentieth century, it occurs seventy-five times, accounting for around 30 per cent of expressions of future time.[28] This is a construction whose progress is likely to be interesting in the next twenty or so years.

Summary

Let us now summarize what we have discovered so far about the spread of a change within a language.

Any change, we noted, tends to start in a small way, affecting a few common words, or words important to a particular subculture. At first, there is fluctuation between the new forms and the old, within the same speaker, and sometimes within the same style of speech. Gradually the new forms oust the old. When the innovation has spread to a certain number of words, the change appears to take off, and spreads rapidly in a relatively short time span. After a period of momentum, it is likely to slacken off, and the residue is cleared slowly, if at all.

The slow beginning, rapid acceleration, then slow final stages can be diagrammed as an S-curve, which represents the profile of a typical change.

Changes do not, on the whole, happen in isolated bursts. One original change is likely to expand and spread to progressively more linguistic environments in a series of related changes. This is known as rule generalization. A series of related changes is likely to appear to future generations as one single, massive change.

An uninterrupted sound change is likely to be 'regular' in that it will eventually spread to all, or most of the relevant words. Regularity, however, does not mean simultaneity, since different words are affected at different times. Nor does it mean regular rate of attrition. A change affects a few words first, then a vast number in quick succession, then the final few. The process is not unlike that of leaves falling off a tree. A few are blown off in August, but the vast majority whirl down in September and October, while a few stubborn remnants cling till November or even December.

We have now looked both at the spread of a change from person to person, and at its implementation within the language. In theory, this could have happened in one of four different ways:

1 sudden implementation, sudden spread;
2 sudden implementation, gradual spread;
3 gradual implementation, sudden spread;
4 gradual implementation, gradual spread.

As we have seen, only the last possibility, gradual implementation and gradual spread, represents the true state of affairs. Changes catch on gradually, both within a language, and when moving from person to person. At first, there is fluctuation between the new and the old. Then, the new form takes over, ousting the old. Changes move outward and onward in an ordered way. Within the language, they saturate one linguistic environment at a time. Within the community, they become the norm among one particular group of speakers before moving on to the next.

Although we have now analysed *how* changes spread, we have not yet considered in any depth *why* they occur. The social factors that we have considered so far are the events which *triggered* a particular change, but they did not necessarily cause it in any deep sense. A foolish skier, for example, may trigger an avalanche by going off-piste and skiing on untouched snow.[29] But he alone did not *cause* the avalanche. The underlying causes were a combination of factors, such as the depth of the snow, the angle of the slope, and the amount of sunshine to which it was exposed. When these reached a certain point, any one of a number of events could have triggered the avalanche; for example, a skier, a shower of rain, a gunshot, a rock fall, or an extra hot day.

In the following chapters, we shall look at the whole question of causation in more depth.

PART 3

Causation

7 The Reason Why

Sociolinguistic causes of change

Phaedrus.... had noticed again and again.... that what might seem to be the hardest part of scientific work, thinking up the hypotheses, was invariably the easiest.... As he was testing hypothesis number one by experimental method a flood of other hypotheses would come to mind.... At first he found it amusing. He coined a law intended to have the humour of a Parkinson's law that 'The number of rational hypotheses that can explain any given phenomenon is infinite'. It pleased him never to run out of hypotheses.... It was only months after he had coined the law that he began to have some doubts about the benefits of it.... If the purpose of scientific method is to select from among a multitude of hypotheses, and if the number of hypotheses grows faster than experimental method can handle, then it is clear that all hypotheses can never be tested....
Robert Pirsig, *Zen and the Art of Motorcyle Maintenance*

For centuries, men have speculated about the causes of language change. The problem is not one of thinking up possible causes, but of deciding which of the literally hundreds of theories which have been put forward to test seriously. In the quotation above, Phaedrus, a scientist, is overwhelmed by the number of possible theories which come to mind in his work on physics. A similar problem faces linguists. As one noted recently: 'Linguists are a marvellously clever bunch of scholars; there is really *no limit* to the imaginative, elegant, and intellectually satisfying hypotheses they can dream up to account for observed linguistic behaviour.'[1]

In the past, language change has been attributed to a bewildering variety of factors ranging over almost every aspect of human life, physical, social, mental and environmental. Half a century ago, for example, we find a suggestion that consonant changes begin in mountain regions due to the intensity of expiration in high altitudes. 'The connection with geographical or climatic conditions is clear,' asserted one scholar, 'because nobody will deny that residence in the mountains, especially in the high mountains, stimulates the lungs.'[2] Luckily this theory is easily disprovable, since Danish, spoken in the flat country of Denmark, seems to be independently undergoing a set of extensive consonant changes – unless we attribute the Danish development to the increasing number of Danes who go to Switzerland or Norway for their summer holidays each year, as one linguist ironically suggested.[3]

Even when we have eliminated the 'lunatic fringe' theories, we are left with an enormous number of possible causes to take into consideration. Part of the problem is that there are several different causative factors at work, not only in language as a whole, but also in any one change. Like a road accident, a language change may have multiple causes. A car crash is only rarely caused by one overriding factor, such as a sudden steering failure, or the driver falling asleep. More often there is a combination of factors, all of which contribute to the overall disaster. Similarly, language change is likely to be due to á combination of factors.

In view of the confusion and controversies surrounding causes of language change, it is not surprising that some reputable linguists have regarded the whole field as a disaster area, and opted out altogether: 'The causes of sound change are unknown,' said Bloomfield in 1933.[4] 'Many linguists, probably an easy majority, have long since given up enquiring into the why of phonological change,' said Robert King in 1969.[5] 'The explanation of the cause of language change is far beyond the reach of any theory ever advanced,' said yet another around the same time.[6]

This pessimism is unwarranted. Even if we cannot consider all possible causes, we can at least look at a range of causes that have been put forward over the years, and assess their relative value. We can begin by dividing proposed causes of change into two broad categories. On the one hand, there are external sociolinguistic factors – that is, social factors outside the language system. On the other hand, there are internal psycholinguistic ones – that is, linguistic and psychological factors which reside in the structure of the language and the minds of the speakers.

In this chapter, we shall deal with three proposed sociolinguistic causes: fashion, foreign influence, and social need. Then in the following chapters we will deal with some psycholinguistic ones.

Fashion and random fluctuation

An extreme view held by a minority of linguists is that language change is an entirely random and fortuitous affair, and that fashions in language are as unpredictable as fashions in clothes: 'There is no more reason for languages to change than there is for automobiles to add fins one year and remove them the next, for jackets to have three buttons one year and two the next... the "causes" of sound change without language contact lie in the general tendency of human cultural products to undergo "non-functional" stylistic change,' argued an American linguist, Paul Postal, in 1968.[7] Another similar view is that random fluctuations occur subconsciously, as sounds gradually drift from their original pronunciation. A theory that speakers accidentally 'miss the target' was prevalent about a quarter of a century ago, popularized by an American, Charles Hockett. Hockett suggested that when we utter a speech sound, we are aiming at a certain ideal target. But since words are usually comprehensible even if every sound is not perfectly articulated, speakers often get quite careless, and do not trouble too much about hitting the 'bull's-eye' each time. As he expresses it: 'When a person speaks, he aims his articulatory motions more or less accurately at one after another of a set of bull's-eyes... charity on the part of hearers leads the speaker to be quite sloppy in his aim most of the time. The shots intended for initial [t] will be aimed in the general direction of that bull's-eye, but will fall all about it – many quite close, some in the immediate vicinity, a few quite far away.'[8] The actual shots, he suggests, will cluster round a single point at which there will be a 'Frequency maximum' (see Figure 7.1).[9]

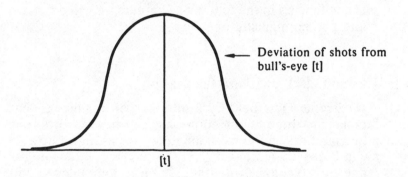

Deviation of shots from bull's-eye [t]

[t]

Fig. 7.1: Hockett's theory of random deviation (based on Hockett, 1958)

As time passes, and quite a lot of shots miss the target, people hear numerous near misses. Eventually they begin to think the bull's-eye is in a different place:

It is just this sort of slow drifting about of expectation distributions, shared by people who are in constant communication, that we mean to subsume the term 'sound change'.... The drift might well not be in any determinate direction: the maxima might wander a bit further apart, then come closer again, and so on. Nevertheless, the drift thus shown would constitute sound change.[10]

How are we to assess these theories? Certainly, fashion and social influence cannot be ignored, as we saw in the case of New York *r*. It is also clear that a person's speech can gradually alter over the years in the direction of those around him, as is shown by British people who pick up an American accent in a very short time. Nevertheless, there are three reasons why fashion and 'wandering targets' cannot be regarded as major causes of language change.

First, if sounds wandered around randomly in the way Postal and Hockett suggest, language would soon end up in chaos. Their theories suggest that sounds are like a room full of blindfold or drunken men randomly weaving and wandering around, and occasionally crashing into one another. Instead, language remains a well-organized, patterned whole, and never disintegrates into the confusion implied by random fluctuation theories.

A second argument against random fluctuation is that similar changes tend to recur in quite unconnected languages. This cannot be chance. If language were purely governed by fashion, we would not expect so many different, far-flung languages to hit on the same whims of fashion in pronunciation over the centuries.

Thirdly, there seem to be hidden and inbuilt constraints concerning which elements can change in a language. There are often identifiable 'weak spots' in a language structure where change will be likely to strike, as well as stable elements which are likely to resist change.

For these reasons, the majority of linguists regard fashion changes simply as a triggering factor, something which may set off a tendency whose deeper causes lie hidden beneath the surface.

Foreign bodies

A viewpoint somewhat similar to the one considered in the previous section is the theory that the majority of change is due to the chance infiltration of foreign elements. Perhaps the most widespread version of this view is the so-called **substratum theory** – the suggestion that when immigrants come to a new area, or when an indigenous population learns the language of newly arrived conquerors, they learn their adopted language imperfectly. They hand on these slight imperfections to their children and to other people in their social circle, and eventually alter the language. Consider e. e. cummings' poem 'ygUDuh':

> ydoan
> yunnuhstan
>
> ydoan o
> yunnuhstan dem
> yguduh ged
>
> yunnuhstan dem doidee
> yguduh ged riduh
> ydoan o nudn
>
> LISN bud LISN
>
> dem
> gud
> am
>
> lidl yelluh bas
> tuds weer goin
>
> duhSIVILEYEzum

This is an attempt, accompanied by a considerable amount of poetic licence, to represent the pronunciation of a typical speaker of Black English in New York. For those unfamiliar with the accent represented, a possible 'translation' runs as follows:

You gotta. You don't ... you understand ... you don't know ... you understand ... them ... you gotta get ... you understand ... them dirty ... you gotta get rid of ... you don't know nothing ... Listen, bud, listen, those goddam little yellow bastards, we are going to civilize them.

(The poem is a cynical comment on racial prejudice. It consists of a monologue, or perhaps a dialogue, spoken by a Black English speaker, who is complaining about the yellow-skinned people around.)

According to one theory, this variety of English ultimately arose when speakers of a West African language such as Mandingo or Ewe were brought over to America as slaves. When these Africans learned English, they carried over features of their original language into their adopted one.

Note, incidentally, that in this type of situation the adopted language does not always move in the direction of the substratum language. Sometimes immigrants attempt to *over*correct what they feel to be a faulty accent, resulting not only in a movement away from the substratum language, but also in a change in the adopted language. Labov found an interesting example of this phenomenon in New York.[11] He noticed a tendency among lower class New Yorkers to pronounce a word such as *door* as if it were really *doer* [dʊə] (rhyming with *sewer*). At first he was puzzled by this finding. When he looked more closely, he found that this pronunciation was related to ethnic groupings. He discovered that it was most prominent in the speech of youngish lower class people of Jewish and Italian extraction, and suggested that we may be dealing with a case of reaction of children against their parents. He points out that the Jewish immigrants who came to New York at the beginning of the century spoke Yiddish. Yiddish speakers would normally find it difficult to hear differences between English vowels when these distinctions did not exist in Yiddish. They would therefore tend to ask for a *cop of coffee*, making the vowel in *cup* the same as the first vowel in *coffee*. Italian immigrants would have a similar problem. The second generation of immigrants, however, would be aware and perhaps ashamed of the foreign-sounding speech of their parents. They therefore made an exaggerated difference between the vowels confused by their parents, so making a word such as *coffee* sound like *cooefee* [kʊəfɪ] and *door* sound like *doer* [dʊə].

Another situation in which the infiltration of foreign elements commonly causes change is when different languages come into contact, which often happens along national borders. Inhabitants of such regions are frequently bilingual or have a working knowledge of the other language(s) in the area, in addition to their native language. In this situation, the languages tend to influence one another in various ways. The longer the contact, the deeper the influence. A number of strange and interesting cases of language mixture have been reported in the literature. One of the most bizarre occurs in southern India, in the village of Kupwar, which is situated roughly two hundred miles south-east of Bombay.[12] Here, two dissimilar language families, Indo-European and Dravidian, come into contact. In this village of approximately 3000 inhabitants, three languages are in common use. Kannada, which is a member of the Dravidian language family, and Urdu and Marathi which are Indo-European languages. These languages have probably been in contact for more than six centuries, since many of the inhabitants are traditionally bilingual or trilingual. The Kupwar situation is strange in that, due to social pressures, borrowing of vocabulary has been rare. This is unusual, because vocabulary items normally spread easily. The inhabitants seem to have felt the need to maintain their ethnic identity by keeping separate words for things in different languages. Meanwhile, the syntax of all three languages has crept closer and closer together, so that now the Urdu, Marathi and Kannada spoken in Kupwar are fairly different from the standard form of these languages, with Urdu in particular having changed. The translation of the sentence 'I cut some greens and brought them' would normally be very different in the three languages concerned, both in word order and vocabulary. In the Kupwar versions, however, the syntax is surprisingly similar, with each translation having the same number of words in the same order, so that each language says, as it were, 'Leaves a few having cut taking I came'. It is unusual for the syntax of adjacent languages to affect one another to the same extent as the Kupwar example, though it illustrates the fact that with enough time and enough contact there is no limit to the extent to which languages can affect one another.

So-called linguistic areas provide a final example of the way in which languages can influence one another over the course of centuries.[13] These are areas in which some striking linguistic feature has spread over a wide range of geographically adjacent languages, which otherwise have little in common. In south-east Asia, Chinese, Vietnamese and Thai are all tone languages. In Africa, Bush-Hottentot languages and the neighbouring unrelated Bantu languages contain a set of rare sounds known as clicks, which involve clicking noises somewhat like the *tut-tut* of disapproval, and the *gee-up* sound made to horses. In India, Hindi and other Indo-European languages share with the Dravidian language family certain unusual consonants known as retroflex sounds, in which the tongue is curled backwards to the roof of the mouth. It seems unlikely that these uncommon features arose coincidentally in the languages concerned, and most linguists assume that they spread from their neighbours due to cultural contact.

The examples outlined above show that the infiltration of external foreign elements can be fairly extensive, and must be considered a significant factor in language change. It is important to realize, however, that it cannot be the *only* factor in any change. This becomes clear as soon as we examine which items are taken into a language at any one time. The infiltration is by no means random. A language is only able to accept foreign elements it is *ready* to accept. Indeed, according to one linguist 'the only role of foreign influence which is well attested is its tendency to accelerate changes which are well under way in a language'.[14]

What does it mean to say that a language must be 'ready to accept' a foreign element? We can best understand this by making a list of the characteristics of linguistic **borrowing**, as it is called. 'Borrowing' is a somewhat misleading word since it implies that the element in question is taken from the donor language for a limited amount of time and then returned, which is by no means the case. The item is actually copied, rather than borrowed in the strict sense of the term.

There are four important characteristics of borrowing. First, detachable elements are the most easily and commonly taken over – that is, elements which are easily detached from the donor language and which will not affect the structure of the borrowing language. An obvious example of this is the ease with which items of vocabulary make their way from language to language, particularly if the words have some type of prestige. In England, for example, French food is regarded as sophisticated and elegant, so even quite ordinary restaurants include on their menu items such as *coq au vin*, *pâté*, *consommé*, *gâteau*, *sorbet*. There seems to be no limit to the number of these detachable items which can be incorporated.

A second characteristic is that adopted items tend to be changed to fit in with the structure of the borrower's language, though the latter is only occasionally aware of the distortion he imposes. An Englishman may well not notice how much he is distorting the French food words, though deformation is more obvious in the case of the British sailors who referred to the warships *Bellerophon* and *Iphigenia* as the *Billy Ruffian* and the *Niffy Jane*. The way in which foreign items are adapted to the structure of the borrowing language becomes clearer when we look at English words which have been taken over by other languages. In Russia, for example, people wear *dzhempers* 'jumpers' and *sviters* 'sweaters', and listen to *dzhaz* 'jazz'. A *sportsmen* 'sportsman' has a plural *sportsmeny*, and a feminine form *sportsmenka* 'sportswoman', which in turn has a plural form *sportsmenki*. Similarly *biznismen* 'someone who deals on the black market' is clearly in origin our word 'businessman', and it has a plural *biznismeny*.[15] Swahili has some even stranger adaptations of English words: *Kiplefiti* 'traffic island' is from 'keep left'. Since Swahili words which begin with *ki-* in the singular normally begin with *vi-* in the plural, we find a plural *viplefiti* 'traffic islands'. Moreover, since a number of Swahili words have a plural prefix *ma-*, we find the English word 'mudguard' adopted as a plural *madigadi* 'mudguards' with a corresponding singular form *digadi* 'mudguard'![16]

A third characteristic is that a language tends to select for borrowing those aspects of the donor language which superficially correspond fairly closely to aspects already in its own. Where France adjoins Germany we find that French has adopted certain German syntactic constructions. For example, French normally places adjectives after its nouns, as *un visage blanc* literally, 'a face white'. On the Franco-German borders, however, French has taken over the German order of adjective plus noun, *un blanc visage* 'a white face'.[17] This particular borrowing has probably caught on because French already has a small number of adjectives which come before the noun, as *le petit garçon* 'the small boy', *la jolie femme* 'the pretty woman'.

A final characteristic has been called the 'minimal adjustment' tendency – the borrowing language makes only very small adjustments to the structure of its language at any one time. In a case where one language appears to have massively affected another, we discover on closer examination that the changes have come about in a series of minute steps, each of them involving a very small alteration only, in accordance with the maxim 'there are no leaps in nature'.[18] This can be illustrated by looking at an apparently massive change which is occurring in Guyanan Creole. Guyanan Creole is in fact based on English, but in the course of years it has moved very far away from it, so much so that many people regard it as a different language altogether. Recently, due to social pressures, more and more elements of standard English are being borrowed into the Creole with the result that in some areas, and in the speech of some speakers, the Creole has reverted to something very like standard English. Derek Bickerton of the University of Hawaii has analysed the small steps by which this is occurring.[19] The verb *to be* represents a typical example. Whereas English has one verb with different forms *am, is, are, was, were,* Guyanan Creole uses different verbs depending on the construction, as in the following sentences:

	Guyanan Creole	*English*
1	mi wiiri	I am tired
2	abi a lil bai	we were little boys
3	abi de til maanin	we were (there) till morning

In the first sentence, the Creole version does not use a verb *to be*, and the word *wiiri* should probably be regarded as a verb, 'be-weary'. In the second, the Creole version uses the verb form *a*, which is the normal word for the verb *to be* when it occurs before a noun. In the third, we find Creole *de*, the normal form before an adverbial phrase such as 'till morning'.

The first stage in the move away from the Creole seems to have been a realization that the forms *a* and *de* do not occur in standard English, combined with a realization that English does not distinguish between three environments in its use of the verb *to be*. Initially, therefore, Creole speakers simply dropped the forms *a, de,* and omitted the verb *to be* entirely, except when this totally destroyed intelligibility. The next stage consisted of learning two of the English verb forms, *iz* for the present, and *woz* for the past, and using them in all circumstances, as in *yuuz a kyaapinta, nu?* 'you're a carpenter, aren't you?' The final stage consisted of learning the correct English forms and where to insert them. This progression is illustrated in Figure 7.2 – though note that the situation was undoubtedly much messier than the diagram would suggest. As in all cases of language change, there was fluctuation initially, with the new gradually winning out over the old.

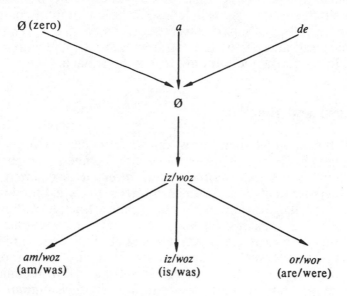

Fig. 7.2: Development of Guyanan Creole towards standard English

In short, we note that foreign elements do not infiltrate another language haphazardly. Individual words are taken over easily and frequently, since incorporating them does not involve any structural alteration in the borrowing language. When less detachable elements are taken over, they tend to be ones which already exist in embryo in the language in question, or which can be accepted into the language with only minimal adjustments to the existing structure.

Overall, then, foreign elements do not of themselves disrupt the basic structure of a language. They merely make use of tendencies already in the language. We may perhaps liken the situation to a house with ill-fitting windows. If rain beats against the windows, it does not normally break the window or pass through solid panes of glass. It simply infiltrates the cracks which are already there. If the rain caused extensive dry rot, we could perhaps say that the rain 'caused' the building to change structurally in a superficial sense. But a deeper, and more revealing analysis would ask how and why the rain was able to get in the window in the first place.

Need and function

A third, widely-held view on sociolinguistic causes of language change involves the notion of need. Language alters as the needs of its users alter, it is claimed, a viewpoint that is sometimes referred to as a **functional** view of language change. This is an attractive notion.

Need is certainly relevant at the level of vocabulary. Unneeded words drop out: items of clothing which are no longer worn such as *doublet* or *kirtle* are now rarely mentioned outside a theatrical setting. New technical terms are coined as they are required, as *tripelennamine*, a hay fever drug, or *Pave Paws*, 'Precision Acquisition of Vehicle Entry Phased Array Warning System', the name of the American Cape Cod radar installation. Names of objects and people are switched in accordance with day-to-day requirements. In a recent novel, garbage at the Board of City Planning in New York was not called garbage: it was called 'non-productive ex-consumer materials'[20] – a new name which was probably coined in order to attract employees to an otherwise unattractive-sounding job. The introduction of slang terms can also be regarded as a response to a kind of need. When older words have become over-used and lose their impact, new vivid ones are introduced in their place. As one writer expressed it: 'Slang is language that takes off its coat, spits on its hands, and goes to work.'[21]

Sometimes, however, social needs can trigger a more widespread change than the simple addition of new vocabulary items. Let us look at two situations in which a wish to express a new concept or a desire for vividness has apparently led to more widespread disruption.

Consider sentences such as:

Henry downed a pint of beer.
Melissa went to town and did a buy.[22]

English, we note, lacks a simple means of saying 'to do something in one fell swoop'. This may be why the word *down* can be converted into a verb to mean 'drink down in one gulp', and the word *buy* into a noun which, when combined with the verb *do*, means 'go on a single massive spending spree'. This type of fast-moving, thorough activity may represent a change in the pace of life, which is in turn reflected in the language, since we increasingly make use of **conversions** – the conversion of one part of speech into another. If this trend continues, the eventual result may be complete interchangeability of items such as nouns and verbs, which were once kept rigidly apart. However, while it is true that conversions are becoming more numerous, there is no evidence that social need initiated them in the first place. Usages such as *Drusilla garaged her car*, or *Bertie upped his score*, have been around in the language for a long time. In other words, social need has simply accelerated a tendency which has been in existence for a considerable number of years. It did not in itself instigate a change, but is merely carrying an ongoing one along a little faster.

A more complex, and perhaps more interesting example of need fostering a syntactic change is found in New York Black English.[23] Consider the sentence *It ain't no cat can't get in no coop*, spoken by Speedy, the leader of the Cobras, a gang of New York City adolescents, in a discussion about pigeon coops. What does he mean? is one's first reaction. Speedy, it appears, means 'No cat can get into any of the coops'. Has Speedy made a mistake, or does he really talk like that? is one's second reaction. We confirm that Speedy's sentence was intentional by noting a number of other similarly constructed sentences. For example, an old folk epic contains the line *There wasn't a son of a gun who this whore couldn't shun*, meaning 'This whore was so good, no man could shun her'. One's third reaction is to ask how such a seemingly strange construction came about in the first place. On examination, we find that it seems to have arisen from a need for emphasis and vividness. Let us look at the stages by which such sentences developed.

We start out with a simple negative sentence such as *No cat can get in any coop*, which was at one time found in both standard and Black American English. However, in order to make the negatives emphatic, and say as it were 'Not a single cat can get in any coop at all', Black English utilized a simple strategy of heaping up negatives, a device common in Chaucerian and Shakespearian English, and in many languages of the world. So we find emphatic negative sentences such as *No cat can't get in no coop*. In the course of time, the heaping up of negatives was no longer treated as an extra optional device used for emphasis, but became the standard obligatory way of coping with negation. Therefore a new method of expressing emphasis had to be found. This was to attach the phrase *it ain't* 'there isn't' to the front of the sentence. So we get *it ain't* + *no cat can't get in no coop* giving Speedy's sentence: *It ain't no cat can't get in no coop*, parallel to a more standard 'There isn't a single cat that can get into any coop'.

Here, then, we have a state of affairs where a need for vividness and emphasis has led to the adoption of a new, optional stylistic device, in this case the heaping up of negatives. In the course of time, the optional device is used so often that it becomes the normal, obligatory form. So a newer, different device is brought in to cope with the need for emphasis – a process which could go on ad infinitum. Note however, that although a new and superficially odd type of sentence has been introduced into the language, it came about by the utilization of two constructions already in the language; the heaping up of negatives, and the use of *it ain't* at the beginning of the sentence. So once again, social need has made use of and accelerated already existing tendencies.

All the changes considered in this chapter were superficially caused by sociolinguistic factors – fashion, foreign influence, or social need. On closer examination these factors turned out not to be 'real' causes, but simply accelerating agents which utilized and encouraged trends already existing in the language. When a gale blows down an elm tree, but leaves an oak standing, we do not believe that the gale alone caused the elm to fall. The gale merely advanced an event that would probably have occurred a few months or years later in any case. However, the gale dictated the direction in which the elm fell, which might in turn set off a further chain of events. If the elm fell against another tree, it might weaken this tree, and leave it vulnerable in another gale. Sociolinguistic causes of language change are similar to this gale. They exploit a weak point or potential imbalance in the system which might have been left unexploited. This exploitation may create further weak points in the system.

Since sociolinguistic causes are superficial rather than deep causes of language change, let us now go on to consider what these deeper causes of change might be.

Note, incidentally, that a number of linguists might disagree with the judgment that sociolinguistic causes are 'superficial' and other types 'deep'. It might be more accurate, perhaps, to replace the terms 'superficial' and 'deep' with the words 'immediate' and 'long-term', which do not imply that one type is more important than the other. It is clear that no long-term cause can take effect without an immediate trigger. It is equally clear that sociolinguistic factors alone cannot set off a change: the language must be ready to move in that particular direction.

Note further that the word 'cause' is being used in the common sense of 'partial cause'. It is sometimes claimed that the term 'cause' should be used only when it produces an inevitable result, as in *Beheading humans causes death*.[24] This extreme sense has not been followed in this book.

8 *Doing What Comes Naturally*

Inherent causes of language change

Thou wilt not with predestination round
Enmesh me, and impute my Fall to Sin?

Edward Fitzgerald, *Rubaiyat of Omar Khayyam*

In the last chapter we noted that proposed sociolinguistic causes of language change were in fact simply triggers, which set off or accelerated tendencies already existing within the language. The gun of change, as it were, had been loaded and cocked at an earlier stage by deeper causes. In this chapter, we need to discuss this notion of deeper tendencies. What are they, and where do they come from? We shall begin by examining some changes which arise seemingly out of the blue to disrupt the language system.

Ease of effort, in the sense of ease of articulation, is the proposed cause of disruption which springs most easily to one's mind. There is a deep-rooted belief among quite a number of people that, were it not for the need to be understood, all human speech would be reduced to a prolonged *uh*. Ease of effort theories have been around for a long time. They were particularly prevalent in the nineteenth century, when educated men tended to idealize the 'noble savage', whose apparent virtues seemed to contrast strongly with the vices and decadence of civilized man. At that time, we find the linguist Max Müller claiming that, owing to a laziness inherent in civilization, sophisticated people do not use the forceful articulatory movements required for primitive tongues.[1] In civilized languages, he maintained, speakers avoid difficult guttural sounds, and show a preference for relatively easy sounds produced fairly far forward in the mouth – a claim which turns out to be totally unsubstantiated, since there is no evidence that any language is 'more primitive' than any other, or that primitive cultures use more 'throaty' sounds than advanced cultures.

A more sophisticated view of changes which are castigated as laziness, however, is that they are tendencies which are inevitably built into language because of the anatomical, physiological and psychological make-up of human beings. As the quotation at the beginning of the chapter suggests, we may be dealing with predestination rather than sin. According to this view there are a number of universal, perhaps innate, phonetic tendencies. Languages tend to revert to their 'natural' state unless a constant effort is made to suppress these natural processes.[2] It follows that, 'phonetic innovation is the failure to suppress an innate, universally natural process'[3] and 'all "new rules" come from a finite set of phonetically motivated processes'.[4] Let us go on to substantiate this viewpoint- by outlining some developments which have happened repeatedly, and are happening currently in the languages of the world.

Final consonants

Let us begin with what seems to be a typical case of sloppiness, the loss of final consonants.[5] First of all, we will consider the reason behind a change discussed in Chapter 6, the loss of final nasals in French, which was combined with the nasalization of the preceding vowel.

Between the ninth and fourteenth centuries AD, French gradually lost *n* at the end of words such as *an*, 'year', *en* 'in', *bon* 'good', *bien* 'well', *coin* 'corner', *fin* 'end', *brun* 'brown'. As noted earlier, this change began with [a], a vowel in which the tongue is held low and the mouth kept relatively wide open. It then moved to mid-vowels such as [e] and [o], and finally to vowels such as [i] and [u] in which the tongue is high, and the mouth relatively closed, In other words, the lower the tongue, and the more open the mouth, the earlier this change occurred. Why?

In the twentieth century, phoneticians have discovered quite a lot about how sounds are produced. Fibre-optic techniques – essentially the insertion of a small camera down the nose – and electromyography – the planting of electrodes in and around the mouth – have led us to a fairly detailed knowledge of the movements involved in articulation. In this particular case, our information has been supplemented by observations of a cancer patient. Unluckily for him, but luckily for phoneticians, he had a large proportion of his face and nose removed. Evidence from this patient, and from the techniques mentioned above, confirmed something which phoneticians had suspected for a long time: when the sequence *an* is pronounced, the nasal cavity – the space behind the nose – cannot be totally closed off during the vowel [a]. The result is that the sequence [an] is always [ãn], with a slightly nasalized vowel. This means that there is an imbalance between [ãn] and the other sounds [en], [in], [on], [un]. There will be a tendency to do two things: first, to omit an unnecessary [n] after [ã] – since the vowel is now nasalized, the final nasal is redundant; secondly, to allow the nasalization to spread to other vowels, in order to preserve the symmetry of the sound system (something which will be discussed further in the next chapter). In other words, any language which possesses the sequence vowel + *n* has a potential weak spot in the language. Starting with *a + n* the vowels may become nasalized, and the final nasal is likely to be lost. We confirm that this is a very common change, and has occurred in the last millennium in Chinese, as well as French.

So far then we have seen that the human inability to close off the nasal cavity during the pronunciation of the sequence [an] causes a weak spot in language which could potentially be exploited. However, this is not the only reason why final nasals (nasals at the end of words) are weak. *All* consonants are weak at the end of a word if no vowel follows. They are weakly articulated, and difficult to perceive. Within the last millennium, the voiceless stops [p] [t] [k] have -been lost at the end of words, in French, Chinese, and Maori, among other languages. In Chinese, they were at first replaced by a glottal stop – a stoppage of the air stream with no sound involved. Then this glottal stop was lost. Several dialects of British English, Cockney and Glaswegian for example, now have glottal stops in place of final [t] and [k], and less often, [p]. So English is possibly following the same track.

This development is not just 'sloppiness', but is due to the general and inevitable weakness of articulation of sounds at the end of words. Let us consider the physical facts behind this occurrence.

The consonants [p], [t], [k] are produced, like all stops, by totally obstructing the air flow at some point, in this case at the lips for [p], the teeth (or just behind the teeth) for [t], and the palate (roof of the mouth) for [k]. The actual articulation of a stop consists of three successive stages: first, the placing of the obstruction, secondly, the building up of compressed air behind the obstruction; and thirdly, an explosion as the obstruction is removed. These three stages can be detected if you try saying slowly and with emphasis: 'You *p*ig! You *t*oad! You *c*uckoo!' Now try saying 'Good nigh*t*! Good lu*ck*! Have a good slee*p*!' Even if you say these emphatically, you are likely to find that the explosion is considerably weaker when [p], [t], [k] occur at the end of a word. Anyone who habitually exploded stops occurring at the end of a word as strongly as those at the beginning would sound both pompous and theatrical. In fact, it is extremely difficult to explode them strongly without adding an extra vowel on the end: 'Good night-a' , 'Good luck-a', 'Good sleep-a'. The difficulty of exploding final stops means that it is not uncommon for stops at the end of a word to be 'unreleased', that is, unexploded. In the phrase 'Good night!' for example, normal breathing is often resumed after the closure and compression stages, without any explosion occurring.

The weakness and gradual loss of final consonants is not only due to feeble articulation. It is compounded and accelerated by the fact that such sounds are difficult to hear, particularly when unexploded. Speakers of Cantonese, a Chinese dialect which has unreleased final stops, were tested on their ability to distinguish between them.[6] When words were read in lists, out of context, hearers made wrong decisions about almost half of them. They perceived 668 correctly, and 520 wrongly, out of a total of 1188. Final nasals produced a marginally better result. Hearers were wrong about approximately one-third: they perceived 845 correctly, and 343 incorrectly, out of a total of 1188.

When final stops have become virtually indistinguishable, the next stage is for them to become *really* indistinguishable. Most Chinese dialects, for example, simply replaced all three voiceless stops with a glottal stop (which, as noted earlier, is a stoppage of the outgoing breath with no sound involved). Eventually, the glottal stop itself tends to be omitted, resulting in the total loss of the original consonant.

Overall, then, it is *normal* for consonants to disappear at the ends of words over the ages. It has already happened in numerous languages over the centuries, and will undoubtedly happen in many more. It is as much of a crime for words gradually to lose their endings as it is for rivers gradually to erode river beds, or rain to wear away limestone. Let us now go on to consider some other natural, predictable developments.

Linking sounds together

When someone learns to write, he at first writes slowly and jerkily, one letter at a time, with each stroke of the pen drawn separately. As he becomes more skilled, he learns to combine and overlap these separate actions. His writing becomes faster and less effortful, and he joins together the various letters. A similar phenomenon occurs in spoken language. When someone learns a new language, he speaks slowly, haltingly, one word at a time, with each section of a word pronounced carefully and clearly. As he becomes more fluent, he learns to link these separate words and sounds together into a smoother style of speech. The jerkiness and unnaturalness of saying words one by one is used to great comic effect by Bernard Shaw in *Pygmalion*, when Eliza Doolittle self-consciously carries her pronunciation exercises into practice in front of a group of people: 'How – do – you – do?'

The linking together of sounds and words is carried out primarily in two ways. First, by assimilation, 'becoming similar': when two sounds are adjacent, one often moves partially or wholly in the direction of the other. Secondly, by omission: in a group of sounds clustered together, one sometimes gets left out. As an example of the first process, try saying the sentences *I want you to warn Peter* and *I want you to warm Peter* fairly fast. At normal conversational speed, there is unlikely to be any difference between the two. *Warn* is likely to have been influenced by the following *p* and become *warm* also. As an example of the second process, say the sentence *George banged the drum hard as he marched through the town*. At normal conversational speed, you are likely to have omitted the final sound in *banged, marched*, and said: *George bang(ed) the drum hard as he march(ed) through the town*. Even people who criticize others for 'swallowing their words' are likely to assimilate and omit sounds in the way described above, though they would probably deny it. As noted in Chapter 5, such phenomena tend to creep into the language unnoticed. Suddenly, there comes an arbitrary point at which people stop ignoring them, and start noticing and complaining.

When assimilations and omissions occur between words, they are usually only temporary: we normally pronounce *would you* as wood-joo [wʊdʒuː:], but the word *you* is in no danger of changing to *joo* in other contexts. However, when assimilation and omission occur within words instead of between them, the effect is likely to be longer-lasting – though the spelling can often prevent people from realizing that a change has occurred. Almost everyone, for example, pronounces the word *handbag* as *hambag* with omission of the *d* in *hand*, and a change of the *n* to *m*, due to the influence of the following *b* (since *m* and *b* are both produced by closing the lips). However, few people will admit to this 'sloppy' pronunciation. Many, when challenged, are convinced that they say *handbag* – though the same people will usually admit to saying *hankerchief*, rather than *handkerchief*. If a change occurs in enough words, people grow to accept it, and eventually treat the spelling rather than the pronunciation as aberrant. For example, no one nowadays worries that we do not pronounce the *t* in words such as *whistle, thistle, castle, fasten, hasten*, even though one might expect people to want to keep *t* in *fasten* and *hasten* in order to retain their connection with *fast* and *haste*. But in this case, it is the spelling which people generally want to reform.

Assimilation and omission then are found the world over, especially when two or more consonants meet. Furthermore, there is some evidence that an alternating consonant-vowel-consonant-vowel sequence is the most natural one for the human vocal organs, and a few linguists have tried to argue that all languages are subconsciously striving towards this natural state. This view is perhaps somewhat extreme, but it is certainly true that fluent speakers in every known language inevitably simplify consonant sequences, particularly if they are able to make themselves understood without pronouncing each sound in detail. As one phonetician expressed it, 'Language does what it has to do for efficiency and gets away with what it can.'[7]

This can seem like laziness only to a real pedant – the equivalent of someone who, when dealing with the written language, prints each letter of each word slowly and separately, and who, like the old lady in Parkinson's Law, is likely to spend all day meticulously writing and mailing one letter. A more realistic view might be that language is simply being efficient. The situation is in some ways analogous to that described in Shirley Conran's book *Superwoman*. How, she asks, can a woman be superefficient and get more things done in her life? The answer is: 'Try cutting out anything which isn't essential. The secret is *elimination*.... Consider these time-savers.... Don't dry dishes. Don't lay a tablecloth or use table napkins. Don't make beds, don't iron handkerchiefs. Don't iron pyjamas or nightclothes.' Language leaves out or glosses over inessential sounds in much the same way. Shirley Conran notes that 'Life is too short to stuff a mushroom'. One might also say that life is too short to put a *d* on the end of each *and*: whether we are talking about *bread an'butter*, *bread an'honey* or *strawberries an'cream* – the *d* is not required.

Other natural tendencies

In recent years phoneticians have built up a fairly extensive list of changes which happen repeatedly. Some are due to the difficulty of co-ordinating a number of articulatory movements perfectly, others to perceptual problems, and others to idiosyncratic effects which certain sounds have on others.

Compare, for example, the word *fambly* meaning 'family' (as in 'I don't recollect that John had a fambly', said by the Oklahoma-raised preacher in Steinbeck's *The Grapes of Wrath*), the English word *bramble*, and the Greek word *ambrosia* 'food of the gods'. At an earlier stage, each of these words lacked a *b*: *fam(i)ly*, *braem(e)l*, *amrotia*. They show that a sequence [ml] or [mr] is likely to change in the course of time into [mbl] and [mbr].[8] This is because it is exceptionally difficult to co-ordinate the articulatory movements involved in the pronunciation of [ml] and [mr]. The lips are closed during the articulation of [m], and the nasal cavity open. If, at the end of [m], the nasal cavity is closed before the lips are opened, by even a fraction of a second, the result will be an intrusive [b]. Similarly, [p] tends to creep in between [m] and [t]: most people pronounce *dreamt, warmth, something, hamster*, as if they were spelled *drempt, warmpth, somepthing, hampster*. Finally, [t] tends to creep in between [n] and [s], so words such as *fancy, tinsel, mincer, prince*, often sound something like *fantsy, tintsel, mintser, prints*. Ask someone to repeat a sentence such as 'Would you recognize the footprints of Prince Charles?' and check if there is any difference between *prints* and *prince*. Your informant is unlikely to make any distinction.

A recurrent change which is sometimes attributed to difficulty of perception is that of 'dark' *l* to *u*. English *l*, when it occurs at the end of a word, or before a consonant, as in *pill, bottle, film, milk*, is pronounced with the back of the tongue raised, a so-called 'dark' or 'velar' *l*. (Compare the 'ordinary' *l* in *lip* with the dark *l* in *pill*.) Dark *l* can sound similar to u^9 – and some varieties of English now have words sounding like *bottu, fium, miuk*, in place of *bottle, film, milk*.

The effect of a sound on its neighbour is seen in the case of *ng* [ŋ] which moves a previous [e] towards [i], as has happened in the pronunciation of the word *England*, which was once *Engla-lond*, but is now uttered as if it was *Ingland*.

These are a mere sample of the phonetic tendencies which are present in all human languages, tendencies which are the inevitable result of a human's physical make-up. Some of them occur invariably whenever certain sounds are produced, others put in an appearance only intermittently. Some of them can be guaranteed to cause change, others wait in the wings, as it were, biding their time until some chance circumstance allows them to sneak in and take hold. Clearly, different languages do not implement all possible tendencies at once, and different languages will be affected in different ways. Something which profoundly affects one language can leave another untouched. For example, it has recently been noted that, the world over, there is a natural tendency to pronounce vowels on a slightly higher pitch after voiceless consonants such as [p], [t], [k], than after voiced consonants such as [b], [d], [g]. This tendency became exaggerated in Chinese many centuries ago, and the exaggeration was followed by a loss of the distinction between voiced and voiceless consonants. The result is that Chinese is now a tone language – one which distinguishes between words by means of variations in pitch. This potential development has been left untouched by European languages.[10]

It can be instructive to look at dialects of the same language, and see which tendencies are implemented, and which not. It often happens that change infiltrates at the same weak spots in several dialects, though each dialect will respond in a different way. For example, it is physically difficult to maintain a single voiceless stop such as [t] when it is surrounded by vowels: these stops have become voiced in American English, where *latter* and *ladder* can be indistinguishable from the point of view of the consonants in the middle. In British English, on the other hand, people sometimes simply cut off the air stream, rather than pronouncing [t] fully, resulting in a glottal stop, heard in the Cockney pronunciations of *bu'er*, *le'er* and so on.

Once a change has entered a language, it can be accelerated, slowed down or even reversed both by social and linguistic factors. A Swedish change which started in the fourteenth century involves the loss of final [d] in words such as *ved* 'wood', *hund* 'dog' and *blad* 'leaf'. A recent survey in Stockholm has shown that there are fewer instances of omitted [d] in the city today than there were fifty years ago.[11] The change seems to be reversing itself, perhaps due to the spread of literacy, which has caused Swedes to take note of the written form of the word which is spelt with *d*. Again, in some dialects of American English, it is common to omit the second of two consonants at the end of words such as *kept*, *crept*, *swept*, resulting in *kep'*, *crep'*, *swep'*. But if loss of the final consonant would result in confusion between the present and past forms of the verb, it is retained: so we find *stepped*, *heaped*, not **step'*, **heap'*.[12] In this case, therefore, a change has been halted in one particular part of the language only.

A similar example of a partial holding back of a natural tendency occurs in French, a language which has a large number of vowels. Four of these are nasal vowels: [ã] and [ɔ̃] as in *blanc* [blã] 'white' and *blond* [blɔ̃] 'fair'; and [ɛ̃] and [œ̃] as in *brin* [brɛ̃] 'shoot, blade' and *brun* [brœ̃] 'brown'. From the point of view of the hearer, these pairs contain vowels which are relatively difficult to distinguish (a fact known by all English learners of French!). The second pair [ɛ̃] and [œ̃] seems, predictably, to be merging. But the vowels of the first pair [ã] and [ɔ̃] seem to be maintaining their identity with no hint of confusion.[13] Why? Perhaps because this pair distinguishes between numerous common words such as *temps* 'weather', *ton* 'tone', *lent* 'slow', *long* 'long'. The other pair distinguishes between relatively few. So once again, natural tendencies cannot be looked at alone, since their implementation is governed by additional social and linguistic factors.

Although slowing down or reversals of changes are possible, as the above examples show, change usually creeps on inexorably, hindered to some extent by literacy and other social factors, but not for long. As we have already noted in Chapters 5 and 6, it creeps in unnoticed for the most part and enmeshes the language firmly before people are aware of it.

Parallel developments in syntax

So far in this chapter we have considered changes made likely by the structure and nature of human articulatory organs, and hearing mechanisms. Let us now go on to look at some more controversial and less tangible natural tendencies, those which involve mental, rather than physical phenomena.

Just as we find parallel sound changes occurring in geographically and culturally separated languages, so we find parallel syntactic changes. Ancient Greek, for example, and certain Niger-Congo languages changed their basic word order in a set of remarkably similar stages. It is likely, therefore, that universal mental tendencies exist parallel to the physical ones which we have already discussed. Such tendencies are more difficult to confirm, since in our current state of knowledge we cannot relate them to the structure of the brain in the same way that we can relate phonetic tendencies to properties of the ear and vocal organs.

Let us consider two possible examples of the type of tendency we are discussing, both of which are present in the Greek and Niger-Congo word order changes mentioned above. The first of these is a preference for keeping the object and the main verb close together in a sentence.[14] This can be exemplified in a trivial way in English. We say sentences such as *Henry seduced Petronella in the woods on Saturday* with a preference for putting the verb *seduce* next to the object *Petronella* rather than **Henry seduced in the woods on Saturday Petronella*. If in English a construction involves an object being moved a considerable distance from the verb, there is a tendency to repeat the object a second time, even though people do not usually realize they are doing this,[15] as in: *Petronella is the kind of girl who when he had arrived in the woods with the primroses blooming and the birds singing Henry felt impelled to seduce (her)*. The final word *her* is put in by a lot of people in sentences of this type, though strictly speaking it is unnecessary, since the object of the word *seduce* is really the preceding *who*, which occurred near the beginning of the sentence. These examples could be paralleled in numerous languages. In ancient Greek[16] and Kru,[17] the most western of the Kwa sub-group of Niger-Congo languages, we find a similar phenomenon which contributed in the long run to a fairly dramatic alteration in language structure. There was a preference for changing sentences such as:

The sceptre which was studded with golden nails he threw down (Greek)
The rice which the child bought he did not eat (Kru)

into sentences which maintain object-verb closeness as:

The sceptre he threw down which was studded with golden nails
The rice he did not eat, which the child bought.

This change was one of a number which weakened a previously strong tendency for placing the main verb at the end of the sentence.

Another, overlapping tendency concerns sentences which have two objects which share a single verb, as in *Aloysius likes shrimps and oysters*, which is, in effect, *Aloysius likes shrimps and Aloysius likes oysters*. There is a tendency in language to omit unnecessary repetitions. Now consider the effect of this on a language which normally places its verbs at the end of a sentence. The 'full' form is *Aloysius shrimps likes and Aloysius oysters likes*. When we omit the repetition, we end up with *Aloysius shrimps likes and oysters* – a deviant sentence in the sense that it does not end with a main verb like the other sentences in the languages. So, in Greek and Kru, we find sentences such as *They were barley feeding on and oats* (Greek) and *He not fish buy and rice* (Kru) at a time when the 'canonical' sentence form required a verb at the end.

In the case of both Greek and Kru, then, a natural tendency to maintain object-verb closeness, and a natural

tendency to delete repetitions, were factors which helped
to destroy the normal pattern of placing verbs at the end
of sentences. Gradually, the verb became more mobile,
and eventually it became standard to place it in the middle
of sentences, between the subject and the object, as in
English.

Ensuing disruptions

Once natural tendencies have been allowed to creep in
and snowball, they are likely to have repercussions on
other aspects of the language system. As we have noted, it
is common for languages to lose consonants at the end of
words. Let us consider some further changes which this
has entailed in French and Maori.

In spoken French, the sequence *chat* [ʃa] 'cat' and *chats*
[ʃa] 'cats' are now indistinguishable, since both the final
[t] and the [s] which used to mark the plural are no
longer pronounced. How then does French distinguish
between singular and plural? The answer is that it does so
by means of the article, *le*, *la*, or *les* 'the' which is placed
in front of the word in question. The article must occur in
French. You cannot say *Cats are stupid* as in English, you
have to say 'THE cats are stupid' LES *chats sont stupides*.
So now we find *le chat* [lə ʃa] 'cat' and *les chats* [le ʃa]
'cats' in which the article alone carries the crucial
singular/plural distinction. Nowadays, therefore, plural-
ity in French is no longer marked at the end of a word, but
at the *beginning*.[18]

In Maori, a Polynesian language, we find a rather
different situation. Here, loss of word endings has led to
an alteration in the way passives are formed.[19] Once,
Maori words ended in consonants, and the passive was
formed by adding [-ia] on the end. For example:

Active		Passive	
awhit	'to embrace'	*awhit-ia*	'to be embraced'
hopuk	'to catch'	*hopuk-ia*	'to be caught'

Active	Passive
maur 'to carry'	*maur-ia* 'to be carried'
weroh 'to stab'	*weroh-ia* 'to be stabbed'

Then consonants at the end of words were gradually lost, so *awhi, hopu, mau, wero*, became the standard active form of the verbs listed above, and most Maoris have no idea that these words ever ended in a consonant. This seems odd, at first sight, because the passive forms, *awhitia, hopukia, mauria, werohia*, have not changed at all. However, if you ask a Maori about the passive, he will say, 'Ah, now passive forms are very complicated, because we have a variety of different endings: *-tia, -kia, -ria, -hia*, and you have to learn which one goes with which verb.'

So Maori speakers have reanalysed the passive as *awhi-tia, hopu-kia, mau-ria, wero-hia*, assuming that the consonant on the end of the verb is part of the passive:

Original construction	New analysis
awhit + ia	*awhi + tia*
hopuk + ia	*hopu + kia*
maur + ia	*mau + ria*
weroh + ia	*wero + hia*

This confusing passive construction is, in turn, leading to an increasing tendency to use *-tia* as the standard passive ending. *-tia* is used with new words, for borrowings from other languages, and also for times when the speaker is unable to remember the 'correct' form. So it seems likely that *-tia* will soon oust the other endings.

With all these disruptions it would not be surprising, perhaps, if a language gradually collapsed under the increasing strain. In fact, this does not happen. Language seems to have a remarkable tendency to restore its patterns and maintain its equilibrium. This is the topic of the next chapter.

9 Repairing the Patterns
Therapeutic changes

> I consider that a man's brain originally is like a little empty
> attic and you have to stock it with such functions as you
> choose.... It is a mistake to think that that little room has
> elastic walls and can distend to any extent.
>
> A. Conan Doyle, *A Study in Scarlet*

Many people believe, like Sherlock Holmes, that man's
brain has a finite capacity. Recent work on human
memory, however, suggests that such a view is mistaken.
A healthy person's memory is indefinitely extendable
provided that the information it contains is well organized, and not just a jumbled heap of random items.

Every language, as we have already pointed out, contains a finite number of patterns. It is these patterns which
enable a human to remember his language so apparently
effortlessly. If the patterns were to break down, man's
brain would become overloaded with fragmented pieces
of information. Efficient communication would become
difficult, if not impossible.

As this chapter will show, language has a remarkable
instinct for self-preservation. It contains inbuilt self-
regulating devices which restore broken patterns and
prevent disintegration. More accurately, of course, it is
the speakers of the language who perform these adjustments in response to some innate need to structure the
information they have to remember.

In a sense, language can be regarded as a garden, and
its speakers as gardeners who keep the garden in a good
state. How do they do this? There are at least three
possible versions of this garden metaphor – a strong
version, a medium version, and a weak version.

In the strong version, the gardener tackles problems before they arise. He is so knowledgeable about potential problems, that he is able to forestall them. He might, for example, put weedkiller on the grass before any dandelions spring up and spoil the beauty of the lawn. In other words, he practises prophylaxis.

In the medium version, the gardener nips problems in the bud, as it were. He waits until they occur, but then deals with them before they get out of hand like the Little Prince in Saint-Exupéry's fairy story, who goes round his small planet every morning rooting out baobab trees when they are still seedlings, before they can do any real damage.

In the weak version of the garden metaphor, the gardener acts only when disaster has struck, when the garden is in danger of becoming a jungle, like the lazy man, mentioned by the Little Prince, who failed to root out three baobabs when they were still a manageable size, and faced a disaster on his planet.

Which of these versions is relevant for language? The strong, the medium, the weak, or all three? First of all, we can dismiss the strong version, in which the gardener avoids problems by planning for them in advance. As far as language goes, we have not found any evidence for prophylactic change. Language does not show any tendency to avoid potential problems. In fact, quite the opposite is true: it tends to invite them, as the last chapter showed. There is considerable evidence, however, for both the medium and the weak versions of therapeutic change. In some cases, relatively minor deviations are smoothed away before any real disruptions occur. At other times, language is obliged to make massive therapeutic changes in order to restore some semblance of order, either because small imbalances have been allowed to creep in and expand, or because previous problems have been dealt with in a short-sighted way, causing in the long run more trouble than might have been expected. In this chapter we will look at some examples of pattern neatening, cases in which the gardener keeps problems at bay by dealing with them at an early stage. In the next chapter, we will look at more dramatic therapy, cases in which early actions have been unsuccessful or have in turn caused further problems.

Neatening the sound patterns

A well-organized gardener tends to grow his carrots and peas in neat rows. Language also seems to have a remarkable preference for neat, formal patterns, particularly in the realm of sounds.

As everybody is aware, sounds differ from language to language. Each language picks a different set of sounds from the sum total which it is possible to produce with the human vocal organs. However, the sounds picked will not be a random selection. They tend to be organized in predictable ways. For example, there is a strong tendency towards symmetry: both vowels and consonants are generally arranged in pairs (or occasionally triples).

One common type of pairing found among consonants is the matching of a voiceless sound (one in which the vocal cords are not vibrated) with a voiced sound (one in which the vocal cords are vibrated). So in many languages, [p] has a partner [b], [t] has a partner [d], [k] has a partner [g], and so on. Each of these pairs is pronounced in exactly the same way, apart from the voicing.

voiceless	p	t	k
voiced	b	d	g

Now consider English **fricatives**, consonants in which the air flowing from the lungs is partially impeded at some point, resulting in audible friction. In the eighteenth century, there were eight fricatives:

voiceless	[f] fish	[θ] thin	[s] song	[ʃ] ship	[h] hen
voiced	[v] van	[ð] then	[z] zebra		

Note that at this time [f], [θ] and [s] all had voiced partners whereas [ʃ] and [h] did not. This is a situation in which we might predict alteration, and one in which alteration did indeed occur – and is still occurring.

Pattern neatening began in the nineteenth century, when a partner was created for [ʃ]. This is the sound [ʒ] found in words such as *pleasure, genre, beige*. The new sound came from two different sources. First, a *y*-sound [j] crept into the pronunciation of words such as *pleasure* and *treasure*. These had originally been pronounced as if they ended in -*zer* as in *geezer*. When this -*zer* changed to -*zyer*, *zy* soon became [ʒ] in fast speech, then was adopted as the standard pronunciation. You can test the tendency of *zy* to become [ʒ] by saying rapidly several times: 'Are *these your* books?' The second way in which [ʒ] crept into the language was via words borrowed from French such as *beige, rouge, genre*, and later *aubergine, garage* and others. If there had not been a 'gap' for the sound [ʒ], we would have expected the French words to be altered to fit in with existing English sounds, as usually happens with loan words.

Now that [ʃ] has a partner, what about [h], the only unpaired English sound? [h] shows no signs of acquiring a mate. Instead, it is in the process of disappearing. It has already been lost in a number of British dialects, such as London Cockney, which has been *h*-less for a long time. Consider Uriah Heep's claim to humility in Charles Dickens' novel *David Copperfield*: 'I am well aware that I am the 'umblest person going. My mother is likewise a very 'umble person. We live in a numble abode'. Or look at items in the traditional Cockney Rhyming Alphabet: *A for 'orses* 'hay for horses', *I for lootin'* 'high-faluting', *N for eggs* 'hen for eggs'. [h] would probably have been lost more widely were it not for the strong and somewhat illogical social pressure to retain it. However, the fight to retain [h] may be a losing battle, since it is not only partnerless, but is also relatively weakly articulated and difficult to hear.

The English treatment of [ʒ] and [h], then, is an example of how language tends to neaten up patterns by aligning the consonants in pairs. The symmetry of vowel systems is perhaps even more dramatic. Broadly speaking, vowels are formed by moving the tongue around the mouth in such a way as never quite to touch anything else, such as the teeth or roof of the mouth, so that the air flowing from the lungs is relatively unimpeded. A major distinction is that between **front** vowels, in which the highest part of the tongue is relatively far forward, and **back** vowels in which it is relatively far back. In addition, **high** vowels are those in which the tongue is relatively high, and **low** vowels are those in which it is relatively low. If we take X-ray photographs of the tongue producing the vowels [a] somewhat as in standard British English *part*, [e] as in *pet*, [i] as in *pit*, [o] as in *pot* and [u] as in *boot*, we can then make a note of the highest point of the tongue as each vowel is made (see Figure 9.1).

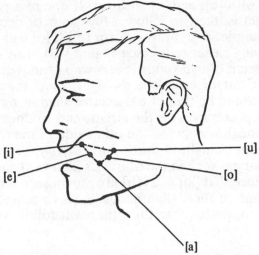

Fig. 9.1: Sketch of tongue position in the vowels [i], [e], [a], [o], [u]

As can be seen, these points form a rough triangle.

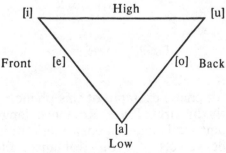

Fig. 9.2: Vowel triangle

Now an interesting thing about vowel systems is that front vowels tend to be paired with back vowels. In a system with five vowels like the one above, [i] will be paired with [u], and [e] with [o]. If one of a pair moves, the other is likely to follow a few years or decades later. For example, if [e] moves closer to [i], [o] will follow suit by moving closer to [u] (see Figure 9.3). The situation is reminiscent of two young lovers who cannot quite let one another out of each other's sight, or perhaps a better image would be that of a detective shadowing a suspect. The suspect moves up the street, and so does the detective, though keeping to the other side of the road, so the two never actually collide. An example of this type of shadowing is seen in the Martha's Vineyard change – it is not chance that [ai] and [au] are moving around together. Once one of these diphthongs starts to move, then it is almost inevitable that the other will follow suit.

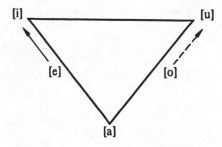

Fig. 9.3: Vowel pairing

A more dramatic example of this phenomenon is seen in the early history of the Romance languages.[1] The various Romance languages each made different alterations in the vowels of Proto-Romance, the provincial Latin from which they were descended, yet each of them maintained parallelism between the front and back vowels. Compare, for example, Italian, in which both front and back vowels were lowered, with Sardinian, in which they were raised (see Figure 9.4).

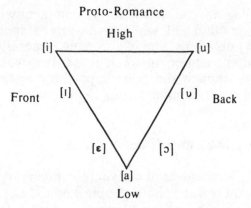

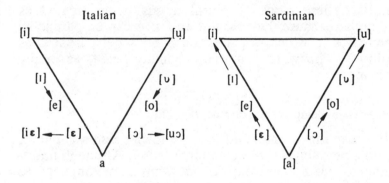

Fig. 9.4: Vowel pairing in the Romance languages

The shuttling around of sounds in company with one another is something of which the average speaker is usually totally oblivious. She is, however, generally more aware of pattern neatening when it involves words and word endings, though she is perhaps likely to treat the phenomenon as disruption rather than therapy.

Tidying up words and their endings

In Chapter 1, we mentioned a seventeenth-century grammarian who complained about people who did not realize that *chicken* was the plural of *chick*, and a twentieth-century journalist who experienced a 'queasy distaste' whenever she heard the word media used as a singular noun. These cases of plural nouns being treated as singular because they did not end in -*s* can be paralleled by cases in which singular nouns have been treated as plurals. The word *pea* was originally *pease*, as in the rhyme:

> Pease pudding hot, pease pudding cold
> Pease pudding in the pot nine days old.

It was gradually assumed that the form *pease* was plural, and a new singular *pea* came into being. Although upsetting to individuals who do not want their language to change, all these examples are part of a long-term tidying process which has been affecting English plurals for centuries. In Old English, there were a variety of different endings to express the concept of 'more than one': for example, *cwene* 'queens', *scipu* 'ships', *hundas* 'dogs', *suna* 'sons', *eagan* 'eyes', *word* 'words'.[2] Over the centuries these were gradually wittled down. First, they were narrowed down to a choice mainly between -*s* and -*n*. In Shakespeare's time we still find forms such as *eyen* 'eyes', *shooen* 'shoes', *housen* 'houses'. Now -*s* is the normal plural, apart from a few minor exceptions such as *men*, *sheep*, *oxen*. (Note that it is slightly misleading to say that the normal plural is -*s*, since it is in fact [s] after voiceless sounds, [z] after voiced ones, and [ɪz] after affricates and sibilants, as in *cats*, *dogs*, *horses*, respectively.)

A similar tidying up process is apparent in English verbs over the past millennium. Figure 9.5 shows the confusing alternations in the parts of the Old English verbs *slæpan* 'sleep' and *crēopan* 'creep', beside their current replacements.[3]

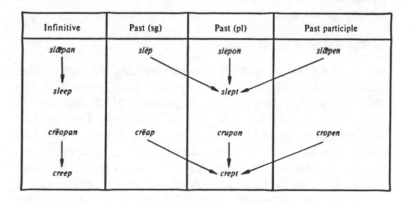

Infinitive	Past (sg)	Past (pl)	Past participle
slæpan	*slēp*	*slepon*	*slæpen*
sleep		*slept*	
crēopan	*crēap*	*crupon*	*cropen*
creep		*crept*	

Fig. 9.5: Changes in the verbs *sleep* and *creep*

This type of neatening is often referred to under the general heading of **analogy** – the tendency of items that are similar in meaning to become similar in form. The term analogy is somewhat vague, and has been used as a general catch-term for a number of different phenomena. It may be more useful to note two general principles behind the pattern neatenings:

1 There should be one form per unit of meaning. For example, the notion 'plural' or 'past' should each be expressed by a single ending, not a great number of them.

2 Alternations in the form of words should be systematic and easily detectable. For example, the rules which govern the formation of plurals and past tenses should be easy to work out by someone learning the language.

In other words, language tends to eliminate pointless variety, and prefers constructions which are clear and straightforward. We find these principles working not only in the case of word endings, as in the examples of plural and past tenses given above, but also in more complicated constructions. Let us go on to look at an example of pattern neatening in syntax.

Simplifying the syntax

As in the case of sounds, people usually do not realize that they are tidying up the syntax. This is because the tidying up often happens by a process of misinterpretation. Let us explain this by an analogy. During her adventures in Wonderland, the duchess throws Alice her baby to look after. It was a queer-shaped little creature, which held out its arms and legs in all directions, 'just like a star-fish', thought Alice. As soon as she examined it properly, she discovered the baby was in fact a pig – and might well have been a pig all along. She had assumed it to be a baby because she had expected to see a baby in the duchess's arms. A similar phenomenon occurs in language. Speakers tend to misanalyse a construction which has become confusing or unclear in terms of a more familiar one with superficial similarities. This happened with so-called impersonal verbs in English,[4] verbs which have an impersonal pronoun as their subject, as in *It ill behoves me to complain*. Such verbs were once numerous, though we now find only isolated examples, as in *It seems that he is ill*, *It happens to be raining*. When these verbs were in frequent use, it was common to put the object in front of the verb as in *Us behoveth furst to pass*, and *Him chaunst to meete upon the way a faithlesse Sarazin*. Soon after the year 1000, however, two changes became

widespread, changes which in the long run affected impersonal verbs. First, endings were gradually lost off the end
of nouns. Secondly, there was an increasing tendency to
use the word order subject-verb-object, which is standard
today, but was not fixed until well after the end of the first
millennium. This meant that sentences such as *Achilles
chaunced to sle Philles* and *The kyng dremed a merveillous
dreme* were misinterpreted as simple subject-verb-object
sentences. In fact, as was obvious when such sentences
began with a pronoun, *Him chaunced to slay Philles, Him
dremed a merveillous dreme*, *chaunced* and *dremed*, and
many others were really impersonal verbs. But, since
these verbs were no longer in line with others in the
language, speakers subconsciously misinterpreted them,
and so neatened the syntactic patterns of language.

Changes which neaten up the syntax seem to be further
examples of the principles already discussed: the tendency
to eliminate pointless variety, and a preference for constructions which are clear and straightforward. Another
common way of expressing this is to say that language
minimizes **opacity** in that it lessens confusing 'opaque'
constructions, and maximizes **transparency**, in that it
moves towards constructions which are clear or 'transparent'.

The examples discussed in this chapter show the extraordinarily strong tendency of language to maintain,
neaten and simplify its patterns. So striking is this tendency, that a few years ago, a number of linguists believed
that simplification was the most important motivating
force behind language change[5] – and a few people seriously wondered why languages never ended up maximally
simple. It has become clear, however, that there are
natural disruptive forces at work, as we discussed in the
last chapter. In addition, attempts by the language to
restore the equilibrium can in the long run sometimes lead
to quite massive, unforeseen disruptive changes, which
trigger one another off in a long sequence. This type of
chain reaction is the topic of the next chapter.

10 *The Mad Hatter's Tea-party*

Chain reaction changes

'I want a clean cup,' interrupted the Hatter: 'Let's all move one place on.'

He moved on as he spoke, and the Dormouse followed him; the March Hare moved into the Dormouse's place, and Alice rather unwillingly took the place of the March Hare. The Hatter was the only one who got any advantage from the change: and Alice was a good deal worse off, as the March Hare had just upset the milk-jug into his plate.

Lewis Carroll, *Alice in Wonderland*

So far, all the changes we have discussed have affected the languages concerned in a relatively minor way. Natural tendencies, exaggerated by social factors, have caused disruptions, then the language has restored the equilibrium again. The situation is reminiscent of day-to-day house cleaning or simple weeding in a garden, when minor problems are quickly eradicated.

Sometimes, however, the problem is not so easily remedied. An apparent therapeutic change can trigger off a set of wholesale sound shifts in which the various sounds appear to play a game of musical chairs, shifting into each other's places like the participants at the Mad Hatter's tea-party. In this chapter, we will give examples of some well-known shifts, then go on to discuss some of the problems surrounding them. The biggest problem, as we shall see, is finding out where a chain shift starts. Suppose we noticed that the guests at the Mad Hatter's tea-party had all moved on one place. After the event, how could we tell who started the shift? The Mad Hatter, Alice, or the March Hare? This type of question has given rise to a considerable amount of controversy.

Famous chain shifts

For the sake of illustration, this section outlines two well-known examples of chain shifts, one of consonants, the other of vowels.

The first example concerns the set of sound changes known as Grimm's Law.[1] These were described (but not discovered) by Jacob Grimm of folk-tale fame in his *Deutsche Grammatik*, published in the early nineteenth century. These far-reaching consonant changes occurred at some unknown date in the Germanic branch of the Indo-European languages, which includes English. They split the Germanic branch off from the other languages, and were certainly complete before our first written records of this branch of Indo-European.

In Grimm's Law, an original Proto-Indo-European [bh] [dh] [gh] became [b] [d] [g]; [b] [d] [g] became [p] [t] [k]; and [p] [t] [k] became [f] [θ] [h] (see Figure 10.1).

The proposed Proto-Indo-European forms are of course hypothetical reconstructions of the language we assume to have existed around 4000 BC, the ancestor of a number of European and Indian languages, as discussed in Chapter 2. Note that [b] was apparently missing in Proto-Indo-European. This seems to be an example of a gap in the system that was filled by all the 'daughter' languages.

A second well-known musical chair movement is one which occurred in the English long vowels. It started around the fifteenth century, and is generally known as the Great Vowel Shift (see Figure 10.2).[2] In this, all the long vowels changed places – though there is still considerable controversy as to which vowel was the 'Mad Hatter' which started this general shift.

These dramatic shifts totally altered the appearance of the languages concerned within the course of

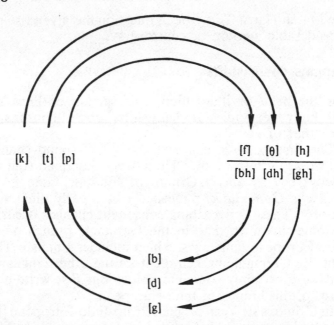

Fig. 10.1: Grimm's Law

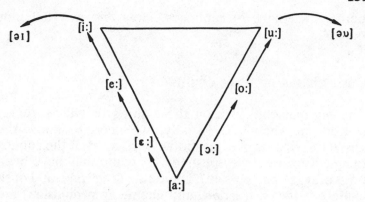

Great Vowel Shift					
Middle English	became	Early Modern English		became	Modern English
[a:] [na:mə] 'name'	⟶	[ɛ:]	[nɛ:m]	⟶	[eɪ] [neɪm]
[ɛ:] [mɛ:t] 'meat'	⟶	[e:]	[me:t]	⟶	[i:] [mi:t]
[e:] [me:t] 'meet'	⟶	[i:]	[mi:t]	⟶	[i:] [mi:t]
[i:] [ri:d] 'ride'	⟶	[əi]	[rəid]	⟶	[ai] [raid]
[ɔ:] [bɔ:t] 'boat'	⟶	[o:]	[bo:t]	⟶	[ou/əu] [bout/bəut]
[o:] [bo:t] 'boot'	⟶	[u:]	[bu:t]	⟶	[u:] [bu:t]

Fig. 10.2: The Great Vowel Shift

perhaps a couple of centuries. How and why did they occur?

Push chains or drag chains?

The big question, in both these shifts, is which sounds started the chain? Essentially, we need to know the answer to one simple question. Were most of the sounds dragged, or were they pushed? Or could they have been both dragged and pushed? The terms **drag chain** and **push chain** (**chaîne de traction**, and **chaîne de propulsion**) are the picturesque terms coined by André Martinet, a famous French linguist, who in 1955 wrote a book, *Economie des changements phonétiques*,[3] which attempted to account for these types of shift. According to him, in a drag chain one sound moves from its original place, and leaves a gap which an existing sound rushes to fill, whose place is in turn filled by another, and so on. In a push chain, the reverse happens. One sound invades the territory of another, and the original owner moves away before the two sounds merge into one. The evicted sound in turn evicts another, and so on (see Figure 10.3).

The question as to whether we are dealing with a drag chain or a push chain, or even both together, may seem trivial at first sight. But since these chains have a more dramatic effect on the language structure than any other kind of change, it is of considerable importance to discover how they work. In recent years, there has been considerable doubt as to whether both types of chain really exist. Most linguists are happy with the notion that one sound can fill a gap left by another, but they are less happy with the notion that one can actually push another out of its rightful place. Unfortunately, we cannot solve this problem by looking at the shifts mentioned above – Grimm's Law and the Great English Vowel Shift. As we noted, Grimm's Law was already complete long before our first written records of the Germanic branch of

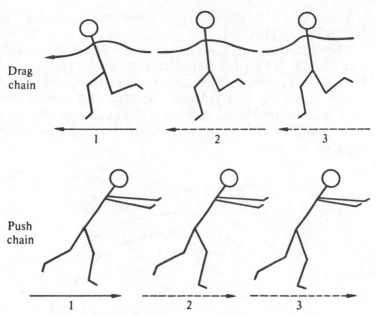

Fig. 10.3: Drag and push chains

Indo-European, and, as far as the Great Vowel Shift is concerned, there seems to have been so much fluctuation and variation in the vowel system from around 1500 onwards, that the exact chronological order of the changes is disputed. Let us therefore examine some better documented musical chair shifts in order to see if both types of chain are in fact possible. This may shed light on Grimm's Law and the Great English Vowel Shift.

We will begin with some sure examples of drag chains, which are relatively easy to find. A notable example occurs in German around 500 AD, in the so-called High German or Second Consonant Shift, illustrated in Figure 10.4.[4] This is called the second shift because Grimm's Law, outlined in the previous section, is generally known as the first shift. It was not nearly as sweeping as the earlier shift, however, and appears to have petered out before completing itself.

Essentially, [θ] became [d], [d] became [t], and [p] [t] [k] became [pf] [ts] [kx].

The chronology of this change has been relatively well established: [p] [t] [k] were the first to change, around 500 AD. [d] changed in the seventh century, filling the empty space left by [t]. Sometime after, [θ] moved into the space left by [d]. So we have a clear example of a drag chain, with sounds apparently being dragged into filling gaps in the system:

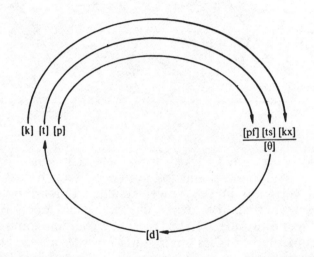

Second Consonant Shift			Modern German		English
[p]	→	[pf]	[pf]/[f]	[pfefə]	*Pfeffer*	'pepper'
[t]	→	[ts]	[ts]/[s]	[tsuŋə]	*Zunge*	'tongue'
[k]	→	[kx]	[kx]/[x]	[brexən]	*brechen*	'break'
[d]	→	[t]	[t]	[tu:n]	*tun*	'do'
[θ]	→	[d]	[d]	[drai]	*drei*	'three'

Fig. 10.4: High German or Second Consonant Shift

	p t k	d	θ
Stage 1	↓ ↓ ↓ ph th kh	↓	↓
Stage 2		t	
Stage 3			d

English, incidentally, did not undergo this second shift, so the English translation of the examples above show the unshifted sounds.

The shift described above is a particularly clear example of a consonantal drag chain, though numerous others exist, from a wide variety of languages, including one in Chinese which performed a complete circle, in the sense that each of three varieties of *s* changed into another, while the overall inventory of sounds remained the same.[5]

Drag chains involving vowels are also fairly easy to find. A change which has been relatively firmly dated is one in the Yiddish dialects of Northern Poland (see Figure 10.5).[6] Here, [uː] changed to [iː], followed by [oː] to [uː].

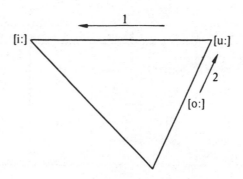

Fig. 10.5: Drag chain in Yiddish dialect of Northern Poland

Let us now go on to consider push chains. Examples of these are harder to find, and some people have denied their existence altogether on the grounds that if [e] became [i], it could not then push [i] out of the way, because it would already *be* [i].[7] In other words, sounds could merge together, it was claimed, but not push one another out of the way. But this objection only holds if sounds change in sudden leaps. Since there is now plenty of evidence that vowels move gradually, it is possible for [e] to move partially towards [i], and for [i] to move away a little in response. It is less easy to see how consonants could behave in this way, and there is not (to my knowledge) a convincing example of a push chain involving consonants. However, a good case has been put forward for a push chain involving vowels in the so-called Great Vowel Shift of Late Middle Chinese, which began in the eighth century AD.[8] The basic movement is shown in Figure 10.6 There is fairly firm evidence that the

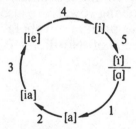

Late Middle Chinese			became	Standard Mandarin	
[ɑ]	[ɣɑu]	'symbol'	⟶	[a]	[xau]
[a]	[ɣau]	'piety.'	⟶	[ia]	[ɜiau]
[ia]	[kia]	'street'	⟶	[ie]	[tɕie]
[ie]	[kiei]	'chicken'	⟶	[i]	[tɕi]
[i]	[tsi]	'purple'	⟶	[ɿ]	[tsɿ]

Fig. 10.6: The Great Vowel Shift of Late Middle Chinese

changes occurred in the sequence shown in Figure 10.6 and over the time scale indicated in Figure 10.7.

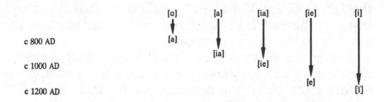

Fig. 10.7: Chronology of Great Vowel Shift of Late Middle Chinese

We may conclude, then, that drag chains and push chains both exist, though drag chains appear to be commoner than push chains. This raises the possibility of whether both types can be combined into one chain shift. Could a chain shift perhaps start in the *middle*, so that it dragged some sounds and pushed others, as in Figure 10.8? Could [e] in Figure 10.8 below be the villain of the piece and *both* push [i] *and* drag [a]? The answer is unclear, though it is possible that the answer is 'yes', since

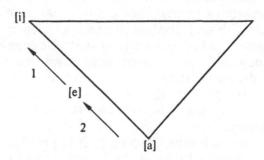

Fig. 10.8: Combined push and drag chain

if Chaucer's rhymes are genuine rhymes, and not near misses, there is some evidence that he sometimes made [e:] rhyme with [i:]. If this spelling reflects the genuine pronunciation, then his work contains the earliest hints of the future Great Vowel Shift, indicating that it perhaps began in the *middle* of the chain – and recent work on the topic supports this suggestion.[9]

Overall then, we realize that this aspect of language change may be considerably more complex than appears at first sight. A simple dichotomy into drag chains and push chains could well be an oversimplification. Perhaps, as we follow through changes in progress, we may end up having considerably more information on these linked shifts. Perhaps by the end of the twenty-first or twenty-second century we shall have sufficient contemporary evidence to compare with the events of the Great Vowel Shift.

Typological harmony

So far, we have confined our discussion of Mad Hatter's tea-party movements to sounds. What about other aspects of language, such as the morphology and syntax (which were briefly defined in Chapter 1)?

Larger constructions seem to be more stable and less promiscuous in that they do not leap into each other's chairs with such apparent alacrity as sounds. However, as we noted earlier, our study of syntactic change is still in its infancy, and there may be more covert leapings, pushings and draggings than we are aware of. Certainly there is some evidence for the existence of a certain type of drag chain in syntax. This involves the notion of **typological harmony**.[10]

As we noted in Chapter 2, it is possible – with some reservations – to divide the languages of the world into a number of different types. Each language type has certain constructions which are typically associated with it. Just as an animal with wings is likely to have claws also, so certain constructions are frequently found associated together in languages. An OV language (one in which the object normally precedes the verb, such as Japanese, Turkish or Hindi) tends to differ in certain predictable ways from a VO language (a language in which the object usually follows the verb, such as English). For example, English has prepositions while OV languages normally have post-positions. So *with care* would be *care with* in an OV language. English places its auxiliaries in front of its main verbs, OV languages mostly do the reverse: so *Archibald must wash* would be *Archibald wash must* in an OV language. And so on. Over the centuries languages tend to alter their basic type. English, together with French, Greek and a variety of other languages, has changed from an OV to a VO language. Mandarin Chinese seems to be moving in the reverse direction, from a VO language to an OV one. When a typological shift takes place, it is not just a shift of verbs and objects, but also of all the other constructions associated with that type. Languages seem to have a need to maintain typological harmony within themselves.

However, in spite of considerable work on the subject, there is no overall agreement as to why this harmony is necessary. One plausible and popular view is that it is related to certain comprehension problems which are likely to arise if the constructions are not in harmony[11] – though difficulties for this theory are posed by languages such as German which involve a strange mixture of different typological characteristics. In German, objects are placed after verbs in main clauses, but before them in subordinate clauses. It is possible – though not definite – that German is in a state of transition, and will eventually end up, like most other European languages, with objects consistently placed after the verb.

There is even less agreement as to the order in which the harmonizing occurs. At one time, it was suggested that the first event was a switch over of the order of verb and object, which in turn dragged round all the related constructions. This has turned out to be wrong. In ancient Greek, at least, the reordering of verb and object occurred relatively late in the chain of events involved in the switch over.[12] In several languages, among them Greek, Latin, perhaps English, Mandarin Chinese, and certain Niger-Congo languages, the earliest changes seem to have involved a switching round of complex sentences – sentences with more than one clause – then only later affected simple sentences and the order of verbs and objects.[13] All we can perhaps conclude at this time is that we appear to have a series of linked changes which are reminiscent of a drag chain, though the exact mechanisms behind these changes remain a question for the future.

Summary

Let us now summarize our conclusions on the causes of language change.

Change is likely to be triggered by social factors, such as fashion, foreign influence, and social need. However, these factors cannot take effect unless the language is 'ready' for a particular change. They simply make use of inherent tendencies which reside in the physical and mental make-up of human beings. Causality needs therefore to be explored on a number of different levels. The immediate trigger must be looked at alongside the underlying propensities of the language concerned, and of human languages in general.

A language never allows disruptive changes to destroy the system. In response to disruptions, therapeutic changes are likely to intervene and restore the broken patterns – though in certain circumstances therapeutic changes can themselves cause further disruptions by setting off a chain of changes which may last for centuries.

Above all, anyone who attempts to study the causes of language change must be aware of the multiplicity of factors involved. It is essential to realize that language is both a social and a mental phenomenon in which sociolinguistic and psycholinguistic factors are likely to be inextricably entwined.

PART 4

Beginnings and Endings

11 Development and Breakdown
The role of child language
and language disorders

The individual organism reproduces in the rapid and short
course of its own evolution the most important changes in form
through which its ancestors have passed in the slow and long
course of their palaeontological evolution.

Ernst Haeckel, *The Evolution of Man*

Many people instinctively feel that child language is of
special significance to the understanding of language
change, perhaps because of the rapidity with which a
youngster alters his speech as he acquires language.
Others have suggested that when dealing with historical
change, we should look also at language breakdown,
again a situation in which rapid alterations occur over a
short period. These are the topics we shall be considering
in this chapter, starting with child language.

Let us begin by dismissing one popular but unfounded
notion, that 'ontogeny recapitulates phylogeny'. This is
the view that change in the language of an individual as
she acquires language recreates the stages through which
the language of the human species as a whole is presumed
to have passed as it developed to its full mature form. This
belief was widespread at the end of the last century, as
suggested by the quotation above from Haeckel's book,
which was published in 1897. Although superficially
attractive, this idea is purely speculative, since the ultimate origin of language is still a controversial and unsolved problem. Alongside those who claim that language
arose in parallel fashion to children's acquisition of
speech, a number of others have claimed quite the

opposite. For example, the Danish linguist Otto Jespersen argued that, 'We must imagine primitive language as consisting (chiefly at least) of very long words, full of difficult sounds, and sung rather than spoken.... Language was born in the courting days of mankind – the first utterances of speech I fancy to myself like something between the nightly love-lyrics of puss upon the tiles and the melodious love-songs of the nightingale'[1] – a view, incidentally, which may not be as crazy as it appears at first sight, since ethologists have recently pointed out some surprising similarities between birdsong and human language.

A second unfounded notion is more modern. Some linguists argue that, even if a child has the same speech output as his parents, his mental internalized grammar will be different. For example, earlier in this century, the words *what*, *when*, *where* were regularly pronounced with an initial *wh* [hw]. Then, in several areas, [h] began to be dropped in casual speech. It is sometimes suggested that the older generation learnt the words with an initial *wh* but possessed a subsidiary rule which said, in effect, 'Delete *h* in casual speech'. The younger generation, however, grew up hearing the simple *w* more often, and so assumed that this form was basic. They therefore had a subsidiary rule which was opposite to that of their parents: 'Add *h* if talking slowly and carefully'.[2] Unfortunately, we have no evidence whatsoever that **rule inversion** (as this phenomenon is called) actually occurs between generations in this way, since we have no means of looking into a child's mind and comparing it directly with that of his parents.

In view of our lack of knowledge on these questions, it seems best to ignore topics about which we can do no more than weave fanciful theories, and concentrate on issues for which we have actual evidence.

There have been at least two serious proposals put forward in recent years concerning the relationship between child language and historical change. The first is the

suggestion that children are the instigators of change –
that all or most changes are due to the imperfect learning
by children of the speech forms of the older generation. A
second overlapping proposal is that inherent natural
processes which cause language change (outlined in
Chapter 8) are present to an even greater extent in child
language. These are the two theories which we shall
discuss in the following pages.

The generation gap

Oh, what a tangled web do parents weave
When they think that their children are naive...

said Ogden Nash. He need have no worries, as far as a
number of linguists are concerned. Far from regarding
children's mutilated words and overregularized forms as
temporary phenomena which get ironed away as children
grow up, these linguists assume that a certain amount of
alteration remains permanently, so affecting the language
as a whole.

This view was popular at the end of the last century.
'The chief cause of sound changes lies in the transmission
of sounds to new individuals,' claimed Hermann Paul in
1880. 'No one has ever yet been able to prevent what
passes from mouth to ear from getting altered on the
way,' reiterated William Dwight Whitney in 1883. 'All the
major changes in pronunciation that we have been able to
investigate originate in child speech,' said Paul Passy in
1891.[3] 'If languages were learnt perfectly by the children
of each generation, then languages would not change....
The changes in languages are simply slight mistakes,
which in the course of generations completely alter the
character of the language,' asserted Henry Sweet in 1899.[4]

Somewhat surprisingly, perhaps, this view has enjoyed
a sudden resurgence of popularity in recent years. Quotations from some modern linguists sound almost like those
of around a century ago: 'We shall hypothesize that the

grammars of adult speakers change, if at all, by minor alterations,' said Robert King in 1969.[5] 'We are led to conclude that the ultimate source of dialect divergence – and of linguistic change in general – is the process of language acquisition,' wrote Henning Andersen in 1978.[6] 'Major changes in language can be viewed as alterations in the set of rules of the grammars between generations of speakers of that language,' claimed the authors of an elementary textbook published in 1979.[7]

Why should this viewpoint have enjoyed such a splendid revival?

The answer has already been partially given in Chapter 3, in the discussion on why so many linguists in the past failed to recognize changes in progress. Let us briefly recapitulate. We noted that, for most of the twentieth century, linguists studied language change by looking at successive descriptions of a language, each one relating to a single point in time. The linguists who wrote these descriptions intentionally ignored fluctuation and fuzziness, and in so doing, eliminated from their grammars all symptoms of ongoing language change. This left them with a problem. They realized that language changed over the centuries, but were puzzled as to how these changes could possibly have occurred, since there was no overt sign of them in the grammars from which they were working. How, they queried, did change take place? One influential group of linguists proposed an ingenious solution to the problem. Presumably, they argued, change takes place in sudden jumps between parent and child. Perhaps each generation of children re-creates a slightly different grammar from that of its parents.[8]

This instant solution seemed to be supported by three separate observations concerning child language. The first observation involved simplification, an aspect of child language which is very noticeable to an adult. It is clear that children simplify the grammar of their language by ironing out irregularities. For example, they overgeneralize regular past tenses and produce utterances such as

Toby hitted me, We goed home, Polly catched it, and so on. As we have seen (Chapter 9), this type of regularization is also characteristic of change in the history of a language. It seemed natural to suggest, therefore, that historical changes of this type were initiated by children, and occur when a child's oversimplified form 'survives into adulthood and becomes adopted by the speech community as a linguistic norm'.[9]

Although superficially plausible, on closer examination this viewpoint turns out to be wrong. At the time when forms such as *hitted, goed, catched,* occur in a child's speech, his vocabulary is still fairly small, and the overregularized forms involve common items of vocabulary. Over the next few months and years, he will be exposed to numerous examples of the standard form of these words, and his own idiosyncratic creations are usually ironed out by around the time the youngster goes to school.

In language change, on the other hand, overregularization first attacks less frequent words, new words, and compound words, which are all relatively unlikely in early child speech. Consider the plural of words ending in the sound [f]. The regular ending is [s], as in *cliffs* [klɪfs], *coughs* [kɒfs]. There are, however, a number of words which retain an older plural in which the singular [f] is changed to [v], and [z] is added, as in *wife* with plural *wives* [waɪvz], *half* and *halves* [ha:vz], *leaf* and *leaves* [li:vz]. People have no difficulty in remembering irregular plurals for these common words. But less common words which once invariably had the old [vz] are now fluctuating. *Oaf* has a plural *oaves* [əʊvs] or *oafs* [əʊfs], *hoof* usually has a plural *hooves* [hu:vz] but sometimes *hoofs* [hu:fs], *handkerchief* has *handkerchieves* [haŋkətʃi:vz] or *handkerchiefs* [haŋkətʃi:fs]. Infrequently used plurals are mostly regular, as *chiefs* [tʃi:fs], *fifes* [faɪfs], *poofs* [pu:fs], *reefs* [ri:fs], *safes* [seɪfs].

Newly coined words are also given the more recent regular plural. Think up a plausible new word, ending in the sound [f], and imagine what its plural might be: 'Buy a *drafe* for your garden! *Drafes* are in this year.' A plural *draves* is possible, but unlikely.

New compounds behave like new words, with regular endings occurring even on well-known words such as *leaf* and *foot* when they form part of a compound. The Canadian national ice hockey team is called the *Maple Leafs*, not the *Maple Leaves*. And we talk of *pink-foots* – a type of goose with pink feet. All our evidence, then, points to overregularizations in language change being instigated by adult or near-adult social groups, and applied to new or less common words which children would be unlikely to know.

A second observation which seemed at one time to support the idea that children initiate changes concerned parallel processes. Certain phenomena which recur in the languages of the world also spring up spontaneously in child language, it was claimed. A much-quoted example is the phenomenon of double negation – two negatives occurring in one sentence, as in *I didn't hit no one*.[10] This is a common construction in the languages of the world, and it also crops up in the early speech of children. English youngsters frequently utter sentences such as *Nobody don't like me*, even when they are brought up by adults who never utter this type of sentence.

However, a closer look reveals that double negatives within child language are not as surprising or as permanent as was once presumed. An utterance such as *Nobody don't like me* is not a spontaneous natural process, but a blending of two similar adult sentences, *Nobody likes me*, and *They don't like me*. The child is unsure whether to place the negative at the beginning, as with *nobody*, or in the middle, as with *don't*, and ends up putting it in both places in the same sentence. This phenomenon is not restricted to negatives. We also find, for example, double tense endings in a sentence such as *Mummy didn't washed it*, which combines *Mummy washed it*, and *Mummy didn't wash it*.[11] This type of confusion is usually eliminated by about the age of five, and has no permanent effect on the speech of those around the child. In language change, on the other hand, double negatives are introduced for more sophisticated reasons, such as the need for extra emphasis (as discussed in Chapter 7).

The third observation which suggested to linguists that children, rather than adults, are the instigators of change, concerned the notion of a 'critical period'. In recent years, linguists have accumulated a certain amount of evidence that there may be a biologically ordained stretch of time for the acquisition of language.[12] Children seem to be programmed to acquire language between the ages of two and adolescence, and any child not exposed to speech within these critical years may have enormous difficulty acquiring it. A number of linguists have therefore claimed that a person's internal grammar becomes fixed and relatively immutable at a fairly young age.

But closer scrutiny shows that the critical period is not necessarily relevant to language change. There is no evidence whatsoever that language learning or language change is *impossible* after adolescence. Those who have argued in favour of the critical period have simply claimed that anyone who starts a language from scratch after that time is likely to be less fluent and have more problems than someone who commenced the learning process as an infant. Furthermore, it is clear that people can and do alter their speech quite considerably in their adult life, as is seen from the case of people who emigrate, or who move to a socially prestigious area, and adjust both their accent and sentence structures to those of their neighbours. Sometimes the adjustment to those around is quite rapid, as shown by an English speaker, recently imprisoned in Delhi: 'Mary Ellen Eather, the Australian, was led through her statement by the prosecution lawyer. After a year in jail she now spoke with an Indian accent . . . .'[13] This girl was certainly long past the supposed critical period.

Overall, then, the arguments in favour of children initiating change turn out to be mirages. Simplification in child language is unlike that in language change, since the former affects common, rather than uncommon words. Apparent parallel processes turn out to have quite different causes. Furthermore, the critical period argument only applies to the fresh learning of a whole language, and not to the partial alteration of an already acquired one.

Babies do not form influential social groups. Changes begin within social groups, when group members unconsciously imitate those around them. Differences in the speech forms of parents and children probably begin at a time when the two generations identify with different social sets. A teenager who tries to imitate his favourite pop singer is hardly likely to speak in the same way as his father, whose speech may resemble that of bankers in the city.

Back to nature

> When I praise your speech with glee
> And claim you talk as well as me,
> That's the spirit, not the letter.
> I know more words, and say them better ...

said Ogden Nash in another of his half-affectionate, half-exasperated poems to children, in this case pointing out the well-known fact that, by adult standards, children mangle the pronunciation of words, saying things such as *guck* [gʌk] for 'duck', *but* [bʌt] for 'bus', *dup* [dʌp] for 'jump', and so on. For a long time, no one thought this phenomenon worth serious study. It seemed reasonable to assume that children could neither hear properly, nor get their tongue round difficult sounds. In recent years, however, linguists have realized that the situation is not as simple as was once thought. For example, a child that says *guck* [gʌk] for both 'duck' and 'jug' can certainly recognize the difference between these words when an adult says them.[14] So inability to hear cannot be such a crucial problem. Similarly, a child who says *tup* [tʌp] and *rup* [rʌp] for 'tub' and 'rub' will probably be able to pronounce [b] in other words such as *but* [bʌt] for 'bus' or *bup* [bʌp] for 'bump'. So inability to pronounce the relevant sounds is not an insurpassable obstacle.

If, in many cases, we can rule out faulty hearing and pronunciation problems, why do children pronounce things so oddly? A view first put forward by David Stampe of Ohio State University is that children are predisposed by the nature of their articulatory make-up to implement certain natural tendencies.[15] For example, it seems to be more natural to devoice stops at the end of a word, so a child will tend to say *dok* [dok] for 'dog', *bip* [bip] for 'bib', and *bat* [bæt] for 'bad'. It is more natural to alternate consonants and vowels, so consonants are likely to get omitted when they occur in pairs or clusters, as in *bup* [bʌp] for 'bump', *mik* [mɪk] for 'milk', *tik* [tɪk] for 'stick'. These processes, as David Stampe calls them; are 'expressions of the language innocent speech capacity', and in order to be able to speak in an adult fashion, he claims, a child must learn to overcome them. He goes on to assert that the natural processes found in child language are the same as those found in language change. He claims, further, that if a child fails to suppress a natural process completely, he can set a change in motion which may spread through the language as a whole.

These claims are superficially enticing, especially as some natural processes found in child language overlap with those seen in historical change, such as the two mentioned – the devoicing of consonants at the ends of words, and the simplification of groups of consonants. But a closer look indicates that the differences between the processes found in child language and language change are greater than the similarities. Let us give examples of some particularly striking discrepancies.[16]

Perhaps the most noticeable difference is the frequent implementation of consonant harmony in child language. That is, when two consonants occur on either side of a vowel, children tend to harmonize the consonants by altering one so that the two are closer in pronunciation, as in *tat* [tæt] for 'cat', where the initial [k] has become identical to the final consonant, or *guk* [gʌk] for 'duck', where the initial [d] has changed to [g] which has the same place of articulation as [k]. This type of harmony can linger for several years, but is extremely rare outside child language. In fact, in language change there is a mild tendency to do the opposite, to make similar consonants dissimilar, as in German *Kartoffel* 'potato' which originated as Italian *Tartufelli* 'truffle'.

Another strong tendency in child language is the substitution of stops for fricatives, as at the beginning of *tum* [tʌm] for 'thumb', *tea* [tiː] for 'sea' or at the end of *mout* [maʊt] for 'mouth' and 'mouse'. In language change, the reverse is more common, with fricatives tending to replace stops, as in English *three* from presumed Proto-Indo-European [treyes].

A third difference occurs in shortened words. Words get shortened both by children learning to speak, and in the course of time. Yet the shortening method differs. Children readily omit the beginnings of words, as in *chine* for 'machine', *raffe* for 'giraffe', *coon* for 'racoon', *mato* for 'tomato', and so on. But in language change, endings are omitted more often, as in *sub* for 'submarine', *pram* for 'perambulator', *métro* for 'métropolitain', *hippo* for 'hippopotamus', *cuke* for 'cucumber'.

Such instances could be multiplied. They indicate that superficial similarities may be misleading. To assume that the processes seen in child language are identical to those in language change may be like assuming that birds and butterflies are the same because they both have wings and eyes. Closer scrutiny indicates that many of the child language processes are due to lack of muscular co-ordination or memory strain, whereas most of the adult ones are due to speedy short cuts executed with excellent co-ordination. Take the sound [p], which is one of the earliest and most stable sounds in child language, but is the stop most subject to alteration in historical change. This is because [p] is easy to produce, but requires time to articulate. A supply of air has to be built up behind closed lips, and then released. If insufficient air is collected, or if the closure is incomplete, the sound [f] results, as is assumed to have happened in the development of the English word *father* from IE [pəte:r].

Overall, then, children have little of importance to contribute to language change – perhaps not surprisingly. Let us now go on to discuss the possible relevance of language breakdown.

Language in disarray

A tree which loses its leaves as winter approaches is superficially indistinguishable from a tree which loses its leaves because it is dying. In other words, this normal change has certain similarities with a pathological one. Similarly, whenever language falls into a misordered or disordered state, it is tempting to suppose that the breakdown shares characteristics with natural language change.

The term 'speech disorder' covers a wide range of phenomena. Here we will look at three broad categories which have intermittently been claimed as relevant to language change: drunken speech, slips of the tongue, and the language of patients who have suffered some kind of brain damage.

Let us begin with drunken speech. Most people agree that this is 'slurred' and odd:

> Out with guns in the jungle stew
> Yesterday I hittapotamus
> I put the measurements down for you
>   but they got lost in the fuss
> It's not a good thing to drink out here...

says Wilfred, the jungle husband, in Stevie Smith's poem of that name. But what actually happens to language when alcohol befuddles the brain?

Two linguists from the University of Texas decided to answer this question.[17] After taking samples of normal sober speech, they proceeded to make their student volunteers systematically drunk. They plied them with one ounce of 'the finest 86 proof bourbon our pocket-books could afford' every twenty minutes for around six hours. Before each new drink of whisky, a subject was asked to read a word list and chat for a few minutes. When they analysed the results, the experimenters found three significant differences from normal speech.

First, drunken speech was somewhat slower, and the slowing down was done in an abnormal way. In general, when speech is drawn out, vowels are lengthened, and consonants remain the same. But in drunken speech, the opposite happens. The consonants are lengthened but the vowels remain the same. In the word *locomotive*, for example, the subject said, as it were, *llocccommottivve* spending considerably longer on every consonant particularly the *c*, though his vowels were similar in length to those in his sober state.

Secondly, the researchers noted that consonants tended to be devoiced at the ends of words: *dog* become *dok*, *bed* became *bet*, *locomotive* became *locomotife*. Thirdly, certain fricatives and affricates changed: [s] became [ʃ], so *yes* became *yesh*, *spin* became *shpin*, and *first* became *firsht*, while [tʃ] and [dʒ] tended to be replaced by [ʃ] and [ʒ] with *church* pronounced as [ʃʒ:ʃ] and *judge* as [ʒʌʒ].

How revealing are these characteristics for language change? There are some overlaps, but not sufficient to regard the two processes as interlinked or parallel. The overlaps are the devoicing of final consonants – possibly a universal natural tendency which we have noted so far in both child language and language change – and the lack of stability of the sound [s]. The main difference is the lengthening of consonants, which happens in drunken speech all the time, but in language change usually occurs only after stressed vowels. Another difference is the lack of

variety in the change of [s]. In drunken speech [s] changes
to [ʃ], but in language change it is equally likely to change
to [z] [r] or [h]. (In change, the alternative adopted usually
depends on the adjacent sounds.)

It is not surprising, perhaps, that drunken speech
should differ from language change. Alcohol slows down
reactions, whereas change often occurs first in speeded up
speech. Let us now go on to look at slips of the tongue.

Slips of the tongue[18]

Interest in speech errors dates back at least as far as 1886
when the linguist Hermann Paul suggested that they
might reveal a natural cause of certain types of linguistic
change.[19] This view of the value of speech errors recurs
from time to time in the early literature on the topic,
though there is little concrete evidence that change ever
starts in this way, or that there is any significant overlap
between speech errors and language change, except in the
case of a few isolated words. Let us explain why.

The majority of speech errors involve more than one
word. Sometimes whole words are transposed, as in *dog of
bag food* for 'bag of dog food', though more often sounds
are switched between words as in *par cark* for 'car park',
or one word alters its sounds under the influence of
another, as in *the thirst thing*, for 'the first thing', *ace,
king, quing*, for 'ace, king, queen'. Sound change over the
centuries, however, involves mainly change *within* individual words.

Any possible parallels between speech errors and language change, then, will involve only those slips of the
tongue which affect a single word, or the fusing together
of two words into one. These fall into three main categories; malapropisms (the substitution of a word for another
which sounds similar), as in 'My wife prefers *monogamous* (mahogany) furniture'; blends, when two words

are combined into one, as in *foreigncy* for 'foreign curren-
cy', and the misordering of sounds within a word, as in
wipser 'whisper', and *relevation* 'revelation'.

Momentary lapses of the *monogamous* for 'mahogany'
type are unlikely to set off a change, especially as the
person who makes an error of this type often notices and
corrects himself. But in character, they are similar to
another kind of error which can sometimes have a permanent effect. These are cases in which a word has been
genuinely falsely identified with another, as in the case of
the old lady who did not realize she had made a mistake
when she talked about 'the Chinese art of *Acapulco*'
(acupuncture).

If two words with a similar sound and some overlap in
meaning get confused by a popular journalist, the new
confused usage can spread, and eventually permanently
alter the meaning of the words. For example the confusion between *flaunt* 'wave proudly, show off' and *flout*
'show contempt for' is now widespread, and used by
influential people such as the press secretary at the White
House, who said that he would not expect the governor of
Texas to 'deliberately flaunt the wage-price freeze'.[20] The
new usage might become confirmed in people's minds by
instances such as ex-President Carter's request to the
United Nations for sanctions against Iran when he stated
that 'The Government of Iran must realize that it cannot
flaunt, with impunity, the expressed will and law of the
world community'.[21] A similar fate is perhaps overtaking
fortuitous 'by chance, accidental', which is sometimes
confused with *fortunate* 'auspicious, lucky', as in the *New
York Times* claim that 'The least fortuitous time to go
abroad probably is with your children'.[22]

The examples above overlap with a process known as
folk etymology. In this, a less common word, or part of a
word, is wrongly associated with another more familiar
word. It occurred in the history of the word *bridegroom*.
Originally, this was *bryd-guma* 'espoused man'. The
second part of the word was popularly linked with *groom*

'boy, lad', resulting in the new word *bridegroom*. A similar situation occurred in the word *belfry* which once meant a 'watch-tower', and was spelt without an *l* as in the Middle English *berfrey*. Since watch-towers sometimes contained alarm-bells, the first part of the word became associated in people's minds with the word *bell*. A modern example occurs in the game of tennis. A ball temporarily impeded by the top of the net as it is put into play is called a *let*, from the old word *lettan* 'to hinder' (a usage seen also in the legal phrase 'without let or hindrance'). But many club players, unaware of the real meaning of the word *let*, have identified it with *net*, and speak of a *net* ball.

A number of other examples of folk etymology can be found among the less educated classes, both in Britain and America, as in 'We have an electric *emergency* (immersion) heater', 'My cat has been *muted* (neutered)'. Although these particular examples recur, they are unlikely to spread throughout the language because their users do not have sufficient influence. However, lower class folk etymologies sometimes catch on, as is shown by historical examples such as *Rotten Row* – the name of several roads in London, which is derived from the French *Route de Roi* 'the king's road'.

Let us now turn to blends. The majority of blends found in the language are consciously coined ones, as in Lewis Carrol's *slithy* for 'slimy' and 'lithe', or the well known *smog* for 'smoke' and 'fog'. A few accidental blends recur in the less-educated strata of society, as in: 'I bought some *rembrandts* (remnants and remembrance) at a sale', 'They gave them a soup *latrine* (ladle and tureen)', 'a *cravat* (carafe and vat) of wine'. But such oddities are unlikely to spread beyond the small group of people who repeatedly say them.

Let us turn finally to the alteration of the order of sounds within a single word. On the rare occasions when it happens, the sounds tend to move in the direction of a more usual consonant sequence. The phenomenon therefore occurs most frequently with names and borrowed words, as in *orang-utang*, from the Malay *orang utan* 'ape man'. A historical example is the word *waps* which changed to *wasp*, though *wopsie* is a dialectal variant still used in some areas.

Overall, then, slips of the tongue are not of any real importance in a study of language change. Errors of ignorance, which resemble slips of the tongue, can set off changes in isolated vocabulary items. But in general, the study of speech errors is of most value in a study of speech production – the order in which people assemble words and sounds for utterance. Slips of the tongue perhaps seemed significant for language change only in the early days when scholars had no idea how change occurred, and made wild guesses about it, attempting to link it with any kind of phenomenon to which it had a superficial resemblance.

Language decay

Disorders which arise from some type of brain damage turn out to be almost totally unlike historical change, above all because speech disorders do not present any unitary picture. Even in recognizable defects, the symptoms are bewilderingly diverse. To assume that there might be parallels with language change is like expecting to get a coherent picture of automobile wear and tear from looking at a series of crashed cars. Furthermore, there is often extreme fluctuation in the ability of a patient from one day to the next, fluctuation that is far more extreme than that found in normal language change.

Even in disorders which are relatively well understood, there are few, if any, similarities with language change. The commonest type of dysphasia (speech disorder) is one in which the patient speaks effortfully and slowly, using mainly nouns and verbs, and leaving out syntactic links between them: 'Why yes ... Thursday, er, er, er, no, er, Friday ... Barbara ... wife ... and, oh, car ... drive ... turnpike ....'[23] This is quite unlike any known type of historical change.

It is sometimes asserted that language decays in an orderly fashion, in the reverse order to the normal order of acquisition by children.[24] This optimistic picture has been shown to be false.[25] The most one can say is that patients with speech disorders tend to have most difficulty with sounds which require the greatest neuromuscular co-ordination, and these sounds are also those which children often acquire late. So both brain-damaged patients and children are likely to replace fricatives with stops, and to have difficulties with consonant clusters – but there are numerous exceptions.

In brief, brain-damaged patients are suffering from a variety of muscular, neuromuscular and mental disorders, all of which impair the normal orderliness and efficiency of speech. Language change, on the other hand, occurs when people whose brains and muscles are acting normally speak fast and efficiently. It would be most surprising if there were any substantial links between the two.

Summary

Overall, language development and language breakdown are disappointingly unrevealing for the study of historical change.

Theories linking child language and language change turn out to be either unproven speculation, or wrong. There is no way of knowing whether change in language as it developed in the human race is similar to child language acquisition, nor is there any means of testing the suggestion that children's grammars differ from those of their parents, even when the output is the same.

The belief that children initiate change was a hopeful guess made by linguists to whom the whole process of change was mysterious. In fact, similarities between child language and language change are largely illusory. Children are unlikely to initiate change, since change is spread by social groups, and babies do not have sufficient group influence to persuade other people to imitate them.

The symptoms found in language breakdown only incidentally coincide with those of language change. Drunken speech contains some of the natural tendencies found in historical change, but it also contains some very different characteristics. Slips of the tongue are unconnected to language change, except in the case of isolated lexical items, whereas the study of language breakdown in brain-damaged people is almost totally irrelevant to the study of historical change.

12 *Language Birth*

How languages begin

> 'Dictionopolis is the place where all the words in the world come from. They're grown right here in our orchards.'
> 'I didn't know that words grew on trees,' said Milo timidly.
> 'Where did you think they grew?' shouted the earl irritably.
> A small crowd began to gather to see the little boy who didn't know that letters grew on trees.
> 'I didn't know they grew at all', admitted Milo, even more timidly.
>
> Norton Juster, *The Phantom Tollbooth*

Most people, like Milo in the quotation above, are quite puzzled about how languages might come into being. When they think about language birth, their thoughts are led inevitably to the fascinating and unsolved problem of the ultimate origin of language. As we noted in the last chapter, there seems to be no evidence either to support or refute the various hypotheses put forward over the past hundred years. If we were trying to choose, there seems to be no reason to prefer the 'ding-dong' theory – which claimed that the earliest words were imitations of natural sounds such as *bang! cuckoo, splash! moo* – over the 'pooh-pooh' theory which suggested that language arose from cries and gasps of emotion. There is also the 'yo-he-ho' theory which proposed that language was ultimately based on communal effort, with essential instructions such as *Heave! Haul!* being the first words spoken, as well as numerous other speculative ideas.[1] We shall not therefore discuss this topic any further, but look at a more concrete and interesting type of language birth, how a new language can come into existence in this day and age.

Since all known human communities engage in talk, and teach their children to speak at a young age, how is it possible for a new language to arise? The answer is surprisingly simple. A new language may come into being when groups of people speaking different languages come into contact for the first time. When this happens, they sometimes bring into existence a restricted language system in order to cater for essential common needs. This restricted system is known as a **pidgin**. In certain circumstances, a pidgin can become elaborated, and grow into a language in its own right. These are the events we shall be discussing in this chapter.

How pidgins arise

The exact definition of a pidgin is a matter under dispute. It is frequently described as a 'marginal' language, used by people who need to communicate for certain restricted purposes. For this reason, pidgins tend to arise on trade routes, for example, along the coast of West Africa, in the Caribbean, and on Pacific Islands. The origin of the term is also disputed, and a number of explanations have been put forward.[2] The most popular theory is that it comes from Chinese Pidgin English where the word *pidgin* means 'business', as in *gospidgin man* (literally *god-business-man*) 'a man who has a god as his business, a priest'. Another theory is that it is derived from a Hebrew word *pidjom* 'barter' – though at least five other origins have been claimed for the word. It is possible that similar terms arose independently in different places, and then reinforced one another, coalescing in the common term 'pidgin'.

A pidgin takes one (or more) already existing language(s) as its point of origin. Many Pacific and West African pidgins are based on English, while a number of those found in the Caribbean are French based. At first sight, therefore, most of the pidgins we know appear to be crude and oversimplified forms of a more sophisticated language. Take Tok Pisin, the English-based pidgin found in Papua New Guinea, which is also known as New Guinea Pidgin, Melanesian Pidgin, or Neo-Melanesian, and which has now been in existence for about a century.[3] Here we find the word *mi* for 'I' and 'me' and the word *yu* for 'you', as in:

mi go	'I go'	*yu go*	'you go'
mi lukim yu	'I see you'	*yu lukim mi*	'you see me'

The plural of 'I' and 'you' is formed by adding the ending *pela* (from English *fellow*) so we get:

mipela go	'we go'	*yupela go* 'you (plural) go'

The English possessive 'my', 'your', 'our', and so on is expressed by using the word *bilong* 'of' (from English *belong*), so we find phrases such as:

papa bilong mi	'my father'
haus bilong mipela	'our house'
gras bilong het	'hair' (from 'grass of head')
gras bilong fes	'beard' (from 'grass of face')
gras bilong pisin	'bird feathers' (from 'grass of pigeon')
gras bilong solwara	'seaweed' (from 'grass of saltwater')
sit bilong paia	'ash' (from 'excrement of fire')
sit bilong lam	'soot' (from 'excrement of lamp')
papa bilong yu	'your father'
haus bilong yupela	'your (plural) house'

Faced with such superficially hilarious adaptations of the English language, some people have condemned pidgins as 'crudely distorted by false ideas of simplification',[4] and dismissed them as 'broken language' or 'bastard jargon', unworthy of serious study. Hugo Schuchardt, one of the few scholars who considered them worthy of attention in the nineteenth century, was warned by a senior colleague that if he wished to further his academic career he should abandon this foolish study of funny dialects, and work on Old French – a warning repeated as late as the 1950s to Robert Hall, an American pioneer in the field.[5] So pervasive was this attitude that only in the last twenty years have pidgins received their fair share of attention. The result of this neglect is that the formation of most pidgins went unrecorded, and the exact process by which pidginization occurred has been lost in the snowdrifts of time. Instead of accurate observation, we have a number of conflicting theories about the steps by which these restricted languages come into being.

The earliest theory, commonly found in the first half of the nineteenth century, was based on the false assumption that European languages are too sophisticated and complex to be learned by supposedly primitive 'natives', who therefore simplified these advanced languages down to their own level: 'It is clear', commented one writer in 1849, 'that people used to expressing themselves with a rather simple language cannot easily elevate their intelligence to the genius of a European language.... It was necessary that the varied expressions acquired during so many centuries of civilization dropped their perfection, to adapt to ideas being born and to barbarous forms of language of half-savage peoples'.[6] This arrogant and naive viewpoint is no longer thought to be relevant. It is a mistake to think that societies which lack western technology have primitive languages. A stone-age culture may well possess less sophisticated vocabulary items, but the language's essential structure is likely to be as complex as that of any other language.

Today, there are four commonly held theories of pidgin origin which are not necessarily mutually exclusive.[7]

The first theory is that of imperfect learning. According to this viewpoint, a pidgin represents the best attempts of a people to learn a language quite unlike their own. In so doing, they produce a simplified form of speech comparable to that produced by children learning to speak for the first time. This is an attractive suggestion and may well be partially correct. It cannot, however, be the sole source of the pidgins of the world, because we have evidence that the Portuguese-based pidgin spoken in West Africa around 1500 was developed by the Portuguese, who taught it to the Africans.[8]

The second theory, therefore, suggests that a pidgin represents unconscious attempts by native speakers of the base language to simplify it in ways that might make it easier for non-native speakers to learn. Such a view regards a pidgin as a regularized form of 'foreigner talk', the sort of broken speech Londoners frequently use if a foreign tourist asks them how to get to the zoo. This viewpoint was put forward by the famous American linguist Leonard Bloomfield, and is found in a number of subsequent textbooks. Bloomfield claims, without giving any evidence, that such 'foreigner talk' is based primarily on imitation of learners' errors:

Speakers of a lower language may make so little progress in learning the dominant speech, that the masters, in communicating with them resort to 'baby-talk'. This 'baby-talk' is the masters' imitation of the subjects' incorrect speech .... . The subjects in turn, deprived of the correct model, can do no better now than acquire the simplified 'baby-talk' version of the upper language. The result may be a conventionalised jargon.[9]

The 'foreigner talk' theory has a number of supporters, although it is unlikely that such talk is based on imitation of learners' errors. There is no evidence that speakers of the base language ever listen critically or attentively to non-native speakers. 'Foreigner-talk', therefore, has its source mainly in the preconceived notions of people who *think* they are imitating foreigners, but are in fact spontaneously creating the simplified talk themselves.

Both the imperfect learning and the foreigner talk theories leave one major problem unsolved. They do not account for the fact that *all* pidgins apparently share certain features. These shared characteristics have given rise to the suggestion that the pidgins of the world ultimately derive from one common source. The main candidate is a Portuguese-based pidgin which was widespread in the trade routes of the world in the fifteenth and sixteenth centuries at a time when Portugal was at the height of its economic power as a trading nation. Supporters of this theory point to Portuguese-based words which are found in a large number of pidgins, such as *save* or *savvy* for 'know', from Portuguese *saber*, 'know' and *pikinini* or *pikin* for 'child' from Portuguese *pequenini* 'little'. Two problems arise from this monogenetic ('single birth') theory: first, it cannot be proved. Secondly, there seem to be pidgin languages with pidgin characteristics based on non-European languages in places unlikely to have been influenced by Portuguese pidgin.

The difficulties of the single birth theory, combined with the observation that all pidgins have common features, have led other scholars to a fourth 'universalist' viewpoint.[10] They suggest that universal language structures automatically surface when anyone tries to build a simple language, and that any shared features will be universal features. Unfortunately, the similarities between pidgins seem to be enormously vague ones, and there is very little that can be said about common language universals beyond the fact that pidgins tend to follow the maxim 'one form per unit of meaning' (Chapter 9) to a greater extent than fully developed languages. A major problem is that any structural universals which might be trying to surface are often obscured by common features shared by the base and the substratum languages. If such a shared feature exists, it is highly likely to appear in the pidgin, even if it is a characteristic which is otherwise rare in the languages of the world.

While scholars argue the merits of these four theories, Peter Mühlhäusler of Oxford University has recently shed considerable light on the origins of Tok Pisin (New Guinea Pidgin).[11] He has shown it to be a product of the particular socio-economic conditions prevalent in the

Pacific in the last century. In its formation, all the above theories may have played a part.

In the nineteenth century, there were extensive coconut and cocoa plantations on Samoa, for which the German owners had considerable difficulty finding adequate labour. Workers were therefore recruited in large numbers from the surrounding Pacific islands. Trading records show, for example, that in the last decade of the century, a total of 1859 labourers were shipped from German New Guinea. Approximately a quarter of them died away from home, but the survivors were eventually repatriated. Altogether around 6000 labourers from New Guinea had a spell of several years on Samoa.

It seems likely that these workers were exposed to a jargonized form of English on the recruiting vessels taking them to Samoa. This broken English probably utilized conventions which had existed in trading circles for some time, such as the Portuguese based *pikinini*, 'child', and *save*, 'know', mentioned earlier. Once on Samoa, this jargon seems to have been developed and stabilized. It was the means by which workers speaking a variety of different languages communicated with each other and with their masters.

Governor Solf's diary for 1895 includes a number of relevant comments on this:

It is a well-known fact that almost every one of the various native islands of the blacks in the South Seas possesses not only one but a whole number of different languages .... Thus, in what way do the workers from such different places and islands communicate, when thrown together in Samoa? They use that Volapuk of the South Seas, which has become international among whites and coloureds: pidgeon English .... The words *belong* and *fellow* are especially important. The former used with nouns and pronouns indicates property, *house belong me*, *horse belong me* 'my house,' 'my horse' .... The latter is added to all numbers, without regard to the gender of the following noun, *three fellow woman* 'three women', *two fellow horse* 'two horses'. It is incredible how quickly all blacks learn this lingua franca ....[12]

Once repatriated to New Guinea, the labourers retained the pidgin they had learnt in Samoa in order to communicate with each other, which was otherwise impossible owing to the estimated 700 languages which are spoken in what is now Papua New Guinea. Whereas the pidgin on Samoa died out as soon as recruiting for the plantations ended at the time of the First World War, the pidgin in New Guinea expanded as it was gradually used for more purposes, particularly administrative and mission ones. At first it was a subsidiary language used when communicating with strangers. Eventually, with increasing mobility of the population, and the growth in importance of towns, it became the first language for children of mixed marriages. At this point it is no longer a pidgin – a subsidiary language used for certain restricted purposes – but a **creole**, an almost fully-fledged language.

Embryo languages

A pidgin is, as it were, a language in embryo. Let us consider its essential characteristics.

First of all, a genuine pidgin must not be confused with broken English, as frequently happens in popular usage. For example, when Paul McCartney was imprisoned briefly in Japan, he claimed that he communicated with the other prisoners in pidgin English, meaning that he used some type of broken English.

A true pidgin has consistent rules. No one can make them up on the spur of the moment. In Papua New Guinea, there is a type of English known as Tok Masta, which is the broken English of certain Europeans who think they are speaking Tok Pisin, but who are in fact merely simplifying English in their own idiosyncratic way.[13] Such people often assert that the natives are stupid. In fact, the natives are simply finding these Europeans incomprehensible. One cannot talk Tok Pisin by simply adding *bilong* and *-pela* randomly between English words, as is sometimes believed.

A pidgin is not made up exclusively from elements of the base language. Vocabulary items are incorporated from native languages spoken in the area, and from others further afield as well. Tok Pisin vocabulary includes, for example *kaikai*, 'food, meal', a word of Polynesian origin, *susu* the Malay for 'milk' and *rausim* 'throw out' from the German *heraus* 'outside'. Constructions are also imported from other sources. Tok Pisin, unlike English, has two forms of the pronoun 'we': *mipela* meaning 'I and others not present', and *yumi*, which means 'I and those of you present', a distinction found in a number of other languages in the Pacific area. Again unlike English, Tok Pisin distinguishes between the form of intransitive verbs (verbs which do not take an object) and transitive verbs (verbs which do), as in the following example using the word *bagarap* 'break down' (from English 'bugger up') and *bagarapim* 'smash up': *ka bilong mi i bagarap* 'my car broke down' (intransitive verb, no ending); *em i bagarapim ka bilong mi* 'he smashed up my car' (transitive verb, ending *-im*). Note also the use of the particle *i* which normally precedes verbs. These examples show that speakers of the base language cannot simply make up a pidgin, its rules have to be learnt. Just as the rules of chess cannot be predicted from looking at the old Indian game from which it was adapted, so the rules of an English-based pidgin cannot be deduced from the standard version of the English language. The pidgin is a separate system, with an identity of its own.

A pidgin is, however, relatively easy to learn. It is simpler than a real language in two ways. First, it has a smaller number of elements. There are fewer sounds, fewer words, fewer constructions. This becomes clear when Tok Pisin is compared with its base language, English. Most varieties of English have a large number of vowels, whereas Tok Pisin has five, [a] [e] [i] [o] [u]. So the words *slip* 'sleep' and *sip* 'ship' rhyme, and so do *tok* 'talk' and *wok* 'work' – and to avoid confusion the word for 'walk' is *wokabaut*. Tok Pisin does not distinguish between [p] and [f], so *lap* 'laugh' and *kap* 'cup' rhyme, and so do *lip* 'leaf' and *slip* 'sleep'. Nor does it distinguish between the consonants [s] [ʃ] and [tʃ], so *sua* means both 'shore' and 'sore'. 'Watch' is *was*, and to avoid confusion 'wash' becomes *waswas*. 'Ship' becomes *sip* and 'sheep' is *sipsip*. Many consonant clusters are simplified, so 'salt' (and 'shoulder') become *sol*, and 'cold' becomes *kol*. 'Six' becomes *sikis*, and 'spear', in many areas, is *supia*.

There are relatively few vocabulary items, so the same word can mean a number of different things depending on the context. Take the words *pikinini* 'child', *han* 'hand', and *haus* 'house'. *Pikinini man* is 'son', and *pikinini meri* is 'daughter' (from 'child woman'. The word *meri* derives from the name 'Mary', possibly reinforced by the word 'marry'.). *Pikinini dok* is 'puppy', and *pikinini pik* is 'piglet'. *Pikinini bilong diwai*, literally 'child of tree', is the fruit of a tree. *Karim pikinini* is therefore either 'to give birth to a child', or 'to bear fruit'. *Han bilong dok* are the front legs of a dog, and *han bilong pik* is a shoulder of pork. *Han bilong pisin* is a bird's wing, *han bilong diwai* is the branch of a tree, while *han wara*, literally 'hand water', is the tributary of a river. *Plantihan* 'plenty hands' is a centipede. *Haus sik* is a hospital, and *haus pepa* 'house paper' is an office. *Haus bilong pik* is a pigsty, and *haus bilong spaida* is a spider's web.

Tok Pisin not only has relatively few vocabulary items. It also has only very limited means for expressing the relationship of one item to another, and of binding them together. For example, English often expresses the relationship between words by means of prepositions, *to*, *for*, *by*, *up*, *down*, and so on. Tok Pisin makes do with only three prepositions, *bilong*, 'of', *long*, 'to', 'for', 'from', and *wantaim* 'with'.

The time of an action is not normally specified, since verbs do not distinguish between tenses, though an adverb can be added if required, as in *Asde dispela man i stilim pik* 'Yesterday this man stole a pig'.

In true pidgins, there is little or no embedding – that is, the combination of two potential sentences by inserting one into the other does not normally occur. Take the statements: *This man smashed up your car. He is my brother.* In English, these would be combined into a single sentence by means of an introductory word such as *who*, *that*, 'This man who smashed up your car is my brother.' In a pidgin, the two statements would simply be juxtaposed: *Dispela man i bagarapim ka bilong yu, em i brata bilong mi*, literally, 'This man smash up your car, he is my brother.'

The second way in which a pidgin is simpler than a real language is that it is more **transparent** (see Chapter 9), in that it is nearer to the ideal of one form per unit of meaning, with systematic and easily detectible rules governing the alternations, as in the forms *mi* 'I, me', *yu* 'you', *mipela* 'I plural' = 'we', *'yupela'* 'you plural'.

The low number of elements and the transparency might make a pidgin seem like a linguist's dream – a near-perfect language. It certainly makes it an easily learnable tool for elementary communication purposes. Unfortunately, such simplicity brings its own problems. One of these is ambiguity. With a simplified sound system and a limited number of vocabulary items, the opportunities for confusion are multiplied. The sequence *hat*, for example, can mean 'hot', 'hard', 'hat' or, less usually 'heart'. The phrase *bel bilong mi i pas* 'My stomach/heart is closed up/fast,' may mean, depending on the area or the circumstance, 'I am depressed', 'I am using a contraceptive', 'I am barren', or 'I am constipated'.

A second problem is that of length. In order to express quite ordinary concepts, a quite inefficient number of words are required. A hymn, for example, is *singsing bilong haus lotu* 'song of a house worship', and a fertile woman is *meri i save karim planti pikinini* 'a woman (who) is accustomed/knows how to bear plenty of children'

Furthermore, the absence of adequate means of joining sentences together creates extraordinarily long strings of juxtaposed phrases, as well as frequent ambiguity.

In brief, true simplicity in a language system is gained at a high cost, such a high cost that it is only feasible in subsidiary, restricted languages. Once a pidgin becomes used for a wide variety of functions, it is forced to expand. It becomes first of all an extended pidgin – a pidgin which utilizes extra linguistic devices and vocabulary items, and which is halfway to being a full language. Eventually, when children of mixed marriages learn a pidgin as their first language, it becomes by definition a **creole**. At this point it expands still further. Let us now go on to consider by what means this expansion comes about.

Creoles as new-born languages

A pidgin is a language in embryo, a foetus with the potential to become a full language, but not yet capable of fulfilling the entire communication needs of a human. Some pidgins exist for a limited amount of time, and then die out. Others get progressively more complex as the purposes for which they are used expand. Eventually there may come a time when the pidgin is learnt by someone as a first language. At this point it has become a **creole**, from the French *créole* 'indigenous', borrowed in turn from the Spanish *criollo* 'native'. The most widely accepted definition of a creole is that it is a one-time pidgin which has become the mother tongue of a speech community: 'A pidgin is no one's first language, whereas a creole is'.[14]

From the point of view of structure, however, it is difficult to know where a pidgin ends and a creole begins, since one can merge into another. There is no doubt that a pidgin must undergo fairly massive changes in order to be viable as a full language, but we cannot pinpoint the stage at which it is mature. All we can say is that around the time of its 'birth' as a creole, it grows rapidly and extensively. Some of the changes seem to occur before it is acquired as a first language, others are initiated by the new native speakers.

Let us look at the kind of maturation which a pidgin undergoes when it turns into a creole. The examples below come from Tok Pisin,[15] which is now the first language for an estimated 10,000 speakers in New Guinea, the commonest reason being intermarriage between speakers of different languages who can communicate only by means of Tok Pisin.

Let us look briefly at four different types of alteration and expansion. The first involves the speed of speech; the second lexical expansion; the third the development of tenses; and finally, the development of relative clauses.

People for whom a pidgin is a second, subsidiary language speak it slowly, one word at a time. When Tok Pisin is learned as a first language, the rate of speech speeds up remarkably. This in turn has a dramatic effect on the phonology. Words are telescoped, and endings omitted. For example, rarely does a native Tok Pisin speaker say the word *bilong*, like the older generation. Instead he says *blo*. So *man bilong mi* 'my husband' sounds like [mamblomi]. The word *long* 'to' is shortened to *lo*, and *save* 'to know, to be accustomed to' is shortened to *sa*. So whereas an older speaker might say, *mi save go long lotu* 'I am accustomed to go to church', a native Tok Pisin speaker would say *mi sa go lo lotu*. To an outsider, the speech of the older generation, the non-native speakers, is fairly clear, but creolized Tok Pisin, on the other hand, sounds just like any other foreign language, an allegro ra-ta-tat of incomprehensible words and syllables.

In the realm of vocabulary, a number of cumbersome phrases are being replaced by new shorter words. For example, the old phrase *bel bilong mi i hat* 'my stomach/heart is hot' meaning 'I am angry' now exists alongside *mi belhat* 'I am stomach/heart hot' with the same meaning. The old phrase expressing a person's aptitude for something by the words of *man bilong*... as in *em i man bilong toktok* 'he is a man of talk, he is a talker', *em i man bilong pait* 'he is a man of fight, he is a fighter' now exists alongside a shortened form, *em i paitman* 'he is a fightman/fighter'. In addition, technical, political and medical terms are being imported from other languages, particularly English.

Meanwhile, it is becoming relatively normal to mark the time of an utterance, even when this is clear from the context. *Bin*, from the English 'been', is now used in some areas to mark past time, even when it is quite obvious that the action took place in the past, as in *Asde mi bin go lo(ng) taun* 'Yesterday I (past) went to town'. The same is happening with the future. *Baimbai* from English 'by and by' was once used as an optional adverb. Nowadays, *baimbai* has been shortened to *bai*, as in the government advertisement for peanuts: *Sapos yu kaikai planti pinat, baimbai yu kamap strong oslem Phantom*. 'If you eat plenty of peanuts, by and by you will become strong like Phantom' (Phantom being a popular cartoon figure who resembles Batman). *Bai* is now often used even when it is obvious that an event will take place in the future, as in *Tumora bai mi go lo(ng) taun*. 'Tomorrow (future) I go to town.'

Perhaps the most linguistically interesting aspect of the creolization of Tok Pisin is the development of complex sentences – sentences with more than one clause. Since creolized Tok Pisin is not yet standardized, different areas have developed these clauses in different ways. The following is a method of forming relative clauses (clauses introduced by *who, which, that*) which has developed spontaneously among a group of families living around Goroka, a town in the Highlands of Papua New Guinea. Here the word *we* 'where' is also used to mean 'which'. The users were perhaps made aware of the usefulness of relative clauses when they learned English, since English is the language taught in schools. The usage actually developed through ambiguous sentences, sentences in which the word *we* could mean either 'where', its original meaning, or 'which'. One speaker, Henni, for example, spoke of the big hospital where/to which all people in Morobe Province go. But in another sentence uttered a few minutes later, she used *we* in 'a way that could only mean 'which'. She spoke of *sista we wok* 'the sister who was working' meaning 'the sister on duty in the hospital'. Her cousin Betty also used *we* in this way. Since Henni is a strong character who dominates those around her, who talks a lot, and whom other people tend to imitate, it is possible that her use of *we* will spread to others in the hostel where she lives, girls who come from different areas.

Time only will tell whether this particular method of forming relative clauses will catch on in Tok Pisin as a whole, or whether it will remain limited to a small geographical area, and then die out. At the moment, there are several independent means of making relative clauses in creolized Tok Pisin, depending on the area. When, or if, Tok Pisin becomes standardized, one of them will win out over the others. Clauses introduced by *we*, as described above, have a good chance of being the 'winner', since this construction appears to have developed independently in other areas in the Papua New Guinea region, for example, Manus in the New Hebrides. Note, incidentally, that relative clauses beginning with the word 'where' are not an exclusively Tok Pisin phenomenon, since they have also reputedly been found in other parts of the world, for example, West African Pidgin, and certain German dialects.

These changes then illustrate how Tok Pisin is developing from a pidgin with limited resources into a fully fledged language.

A creole is a 'real' language in the sense that it is often the only language of those who learn it as their mother tongue. It therefore has to be capable of dealing with a greater range of communication needs than a pidgin. At first, it will be in a relatively immature state, and the language is likely to develop fast during the first two generations of creole speakers. Later, its rate of growth will slow down, as it becomes a fully mature language. In time, it will be a 'normal' language, which takes its place among the thousands of others spoken in the world. It is possible that some of today's best known languages started out as creolized pidgins. It has even been suggested that the Germanic branch of the Indo-European language family, which includes English, German and Dutch, started out as a pidginized version of Indo-European. This startling theory is not generally accepted, but it does emphasize the fact that in the long run there is no way of distinguishing one-time pidgins and creoles from any other language.

Summary

Although the stages through which a new language develops are only just beginning to be understood, the general outline is clear. When groups of people with no common language need to communicate about essential needs, a simplified language known as a pidgin comes into being, ultimately based on an already existing language. The notions of imperfect learning, foreigner talk, influence from an old Portuguese pidgin, and language universals have all been proposed to explain the process by which a pidgin is formed. The early development of Tok Pisin on the Samoan plantations shows that all these theories may be relevant to some extent.

A pidgin is not merely a broken form of the base language, but a language system with rules of its own. It is simpler than a fully-fledged language in that it contains fewer elements, and is more transparent. It suffers from the corresponding disadvantages of ambiguity and inability to express a wide range of concepts easily.

If a pidgin becomes used in an increasing number of situations, the system is expanded and extended. If children learn an extended pidgin as a first language, it has become a creole. At this point it goes into a rapid phase of development which affects all aspects of the language.

Finally, a creole which has been in use for a number of generations will be indistinguishable from any other language.

13 *Language Death*

How languages end

I am always sorry when any language is lost, because
languages are the pedigree of nations.
Samuel Johnson, *Letter to Boswell*

In the nineteenth century, scholars frequently talked
about languages as if they were organic entities, such as
plants, which went through a predictable life cycle of
birth, infancy, maturation, then gradual decay and death.
In 1827, the German scholar Franz Bopp claimed that
'Languages are to be considered organic natural bodies,
which are formed according to fixed laws, develop as
possessing an inner principle of life, and gradually die out
because they do not understand themselves any longer,
and therefore cast off or mutilate their members or
forms.'[1]

In the twentieth century, we no longer have this simple
belief that languages behave like beans or chrysanthe-
mums, living out their allotted life, and fading away in
due course. It is, however, a fact that languages sometimes die out. This is the process which we shall be
discussing in this chapter.

Note that when we talk about languages dying, we are
not referring to languages which gradually alter their form
over the centuries, and in so doing possibly change their
names. Latin, for example, is sometimes spoken of as a
'dead' language, because nobody today speaks it. But it
did not really die, it merely changed its appearance and
name, since French, Spanish, Italian and Sardinian are all
direct descendants of Latin and are in a sense the same
language. By language death then, we do not simply mean

this gradual alteration over time. We are referring to a more dramatic and less normal event, the total disappearance of a language.

Human beings never stop talking. How then can a language die out? When a language dies, it is not because a community has forgotten how to speak, but because another language has gradually ousted the old one as the dominant language, for political and social reasons. Typically, a younger generation will learn an 'old' language from their parents as a mother tongue, but will be exposed from a young age to another more fashionable and socially useful language at school.

In this situation, one of two things is liable to happen. The first possibility is that speakers of the old language will continue speaking it, but will gradually import forms and constructions from the socially dominant language, until the old one is no longer identifiable as a separate language. This is in reality an extreme form of borrowing. The language concerned seems to commit suicide. It slowly demolishes itself by bringing in more and more forms from the prestige language, until it destroys its own identity.

The second possibility is more dramatic. In some circumstances, the old language simply disappears. We are dealing not so much with the natural passing away of a language, as a case of murder – murder by the dominant language as it gradually suppresses and ousts the subsidiary one. Let us look at these two phenomena.

Language suicide

Language suicide occurs most commonly when two languages are fairly similar to one another. In this situation, it is extremely easy for the less prestigious one to borrow vocabulary, constructions and sounds from the one with greater social approval. In the long run, it may obliterate itself entirely in the process.

The best known cases of language suicide are those in which a developing language, a creole, gets devoured by its parent. A creole is often situated geographically in an area where people still speak the language from which it was ultimately derived. Since the base language is usually the one with social prestige, there is likely to be pressure on the speakers of the creole to move it back in the direction of the base. This process is known as **decreolization.**

Decreolization begins, as with other cases of borrowing, in constructions and sounds in which there is an overlap between the base language and the creole and, like all language change, it occurs in a series of small steps.

The phenomenon has been studied in most depth by Derek Bickerton,[2] whose work has already been mentioned in Chapter 7. He has charted the progress of a number of changes occurring in Bushlot, a Guyanan village which contains approximately 1500 inhabitants of East Indian origin.[3] These are the descendants of labourers brought from India in the nineteenth century, who learnt a pidgin English from African field hands, which has developed into what is today known as Guyanan Creole. This creole is gradually becoming decreolized as it moves back towards English in a series of step-by-step changes. For example, among 'deep-creole' speakers, the word *fi* or *fu* is used where English would use *to*:

Tshap no noo wa *fu* du.
Chap – not – know – what – do – do.
'The fellow didn't know what to do.'

In less deep creole the word *tu* is used:

Faama na noo wat *tu* duu.
Farmer – not – know – what – to – do.
'The farmer didn't know what to do.'

At first sight, the alternation between *fu* and *tu* seems to be chaotic, since both forms can occur in one person's speech in the same conversation. Closer inspection shows that, where *tu* is replacing *fu*, it is doing so in an orderly fashion, working through the verb system in three stages. At each step, there is fluctuation between *fu* and *tu*, with *tu* gradually winning out. First, *tu* is introduced after ordinary verbs, such as *ron* 'run', *kom* 'come', *wok* 'work', as in:

Jan *wok tu* mek moni.
'John works to make money.'

As a second stage, it begins to occur after verbs expressing wanting, or desire (known as desiderative verbs):

Jan *won tu* mek moni.
'John wants to make money.'

Finally, it spreads to verbs meaning 'start' or 'begin' (so-called inceptive verbs), as in:

Jan *staat tu* mek moni.
'John started to make money.'

This change, then, moves onward and outward, like other linguistic changes, saturating each linguistic environment in turn (Chapter 7).

Decreolization is also occurring in urban varieties of Tok Pisin.[4] In Papua New Guinea towns, English is the language of instruction used in universities, and the language of commerce and business establishments such as banks. In these environments, Tok Pisin is being increasingly swamped by English words and constructions – a fact sometimes resented by rural speakers. In a letter to *Wantok*, a Tok Pisin newspaper, one rural dweller complained bitterly about this happening: 'Nongut yumi hambak nambaut na bagarapim tokples bilong yumi olsem' – 'We must not [literally, 'It is no good for us to'] mess around and ruin the language of our country in this way.'[5]

Massive vocabulary borrowing is the most superficially noticeable aspect of decreolization in Tok Pisin. Since many existing pidgin words are based on English ones, the mechanisms of adaptation are well understood by the speakers, and hundreds more can easily infiltrate, particularly in situations in which Tok Pisin lacks sufficient vocabulary of its own. For example, Tok Pisin is now the official language of parliamentary transactions in the House of Assembly in the capital, Port Moresby. Political crises require heavy borrowing from English, since Tok Pisin does not have the technical terms to cope. The following is an extract from a radio broadcast[6] describing a change of government:

Lida bilong oposisen bipo, Mista Iambakey Okuk, i kirap na go muvim dispela mosin ov nou konfidens long praim minista, Mista Somare. Tasol memba bilong Menyama, Mista Neville Bourne, i singaut long point ov oda na tokim palamen olsem dispela mosin i no bihainim gud standing oda bilong palamen na konstitusin bilong kantri.

The previous leader of the opposition, Mr Iambakey Okuk, stood up and proceeded to move this motion of no confidence in the prime minister, Mr Somare. But the member for Menyama, Mr Neville Bourne, called out on a point of order and told parliament that this motion was not in accordance with the standing orders of parliament and the constitution of the country.

In the passage above, English structures are imported, as well as English words and phrases, as in *na tokim palamen olsem* 'and told parliament that'.

Advertisements, which often advocate Australian products, also tend to be direct translations of English ones:

Bilong lukautim gud gras long hed bilong yu na rausim ol laus, traim Pretty Hair. Pastaim tru, wasim gras long wara, bihain putim Pretty Hair pauda. Usim wanpela liklik paket Pretty Hair olsem tede, wet inap de bihain long tumora, na usim gen.... [7]

To look after your hair properly and get rid of the lice, try Pretty Hair. First of all, wet your hair with water, then apply Pretty Hair powder. Use one little packet of Pretty Hair in this way today, wait until the day after tomorrow, and use it again....

Rural pidgin would have a number of differences. For example, it would probably use the pidgin word *haptumora* instead of the English based *de bihain long tumora* 'day after tomorrow'.

Expressions of time, as in the passage above, is the aspect of English which has most obviously influenced urban pidgin. Many English phrases crop up, even when a speaker is convinced that he is speaking 'pure' pidgin. This is a continuation of a movement which has been going on in pidgin for some time. Nowadays, even rural speakers tend to say *foa klok*, *hapas tri*, 'four o'clock', 'half-past three', and so on, instead of the more cumbersom pidgin phrases which describe the position of the sun or the amount of natural light, as in *taim bilong san i godaun* 'the time of the sun going down', which is around six o'clock in the evening. In addition, for dates, the English system of weeks and months has been imported. The days of the week are derived from the English ones. *Sande*, *Mande*, *Tunde* 'Sunday, Monday, Tuesday', and so on, and so are the words *wik* 'week' and *yia* 'year'. In these circumstances, it is extremely easy for more English words and phrases to creep in, especially as most urban speakers have a reasonable knowledge of English. So we find expressions such as *fes yia* 'first year' instead of the older *namba wan yia*, beside an already existing pidgin *las yia* 'last year'. The pidgin *sampela taim* 'sometimes' tends to be shortened to the English-based *samtaim(s)*. Phrases and words such as *next morning*, *weekend*, *late*, *early*, *ten o'clock* (instead of *ten klok*) frequently creep into conversations. As in all language change, there is a tremendous amount of fluctuation. On one day a person might use an English phrase, on another day a Tok Pisin one. Sometimes English and Tok Pisin forms of the same word occur in a single sentence, as in *sampela taim mipela goaut o samtaims mipela stap na stori.* 'Sometimes we go out, or *sometimes* we stay in and chat.' At other times, Tok Pisin and English phrases get mixed together. The Tok Pisin for 'first... then...' is *pastaim... bihain...* (as in the Pretty Hair advertisement quoted above, 'First wet your hair... then apply Pretty Hair'). One informant was completely inconsistent over this. Sometimes she used the expected *pastaim... bihain,* at other times the English *fest* 'first'... *afte* 'after'. Sometimes she mixed the two, as in *Fest mi boilim pitpit,... bihain mi putim banana insait.* 'First I boil the pitpit... then I put the banana in.' This girl also once confused *pastaim* and *fest* into a single word, producing the hybrid *festaim. Festaim mipela go kisim paiawut.* 'First we go and get firewood.'

In some sentences, the English and Tok Pisin are so inextricably mixed that it is hard to tell which language is being spoken, as in *Krismas bilong mi, em eighteen years old.* 'My Christmases, it's eighteen years old.' The true Tok Pisin form would have been *mi gat wanpela ten et krismas,* or literally 'I have one ten and eight Christmases'.

These expressions of time represent more than the importation of isolated vocabulary items. Many of them have a more insidious effect. For example, Tok Pisin does not normally alter the form of a word when it is plural. Instead, a numeral is added to the front, as in *tripela pik, planti pik* 'three pigs', 'many pigs'. But in expressions of time, English -*s* is frequently inadvertently added, as in *tu wiks moa* 'two weeks more', *tri des* 'three days', *wan an haf auas* 'one and a half hours', *wikends* 'weekends'. This creeping in of -*s* plurals may represent the first slow stages of a much wider change in the formation of plurals.

Expressions of time are also having an effect on the sound patterns of the language. For example, the increasing use of the words *after* and *afternoon* means that many people now feel *ft* to be a normal combination of sounds in the middle of a word, even though previously it did not exist, as is shown by the pidgin word *apinun* 'afternoon'.

Time expressions are by no means the only aspect of English which is infiltrating the speech of the average urban speaker, though they are perhaps the most pervasive. Numerous other aspects of English life are insidiously making their way into Tok Pisin, and disrupting its structures and vocabulary. For example, most shops and businesses are structured in accordance with the meal breaks in a standard Australian day, so pidgin speakers talk about *hevim brekfas*, *lunch*, *tea*, *dinner* and so on. This, incidentally, sometimes angers older speakers who boast that in their youth they used to work all day without stopping to eat.

Western foods are being introduced alongside the traditional root vegetables such as yam, taro, sweet potato, which used to comprise the total diet of many Papua New Guineans. So people now talk about *mekim sandwich*, *bread*, as in *favourite kaikai bilong mi, em bread, toasted bread* 'my favourite food is bread, toasted bread', *kiau na bread slice* 'eggs and a slice of bread'. As can be seen, this is another area in which western words and phrases have become totally mixed with Tok Pisin ones.

The interweaving of English and Tok Pisin occurs not only in single sentences, but also in conversations. One person may ask a question in English, and the other reply in Tok Pisin:

Speaker A Have you seen our brush?
Speaker B Mi no lukim. (No, I haven't seen it.)
Speaker C It might be in the bathroom.
Speaker A Yes, em i stap. (Yes, here it is.)

The fact that this mixture is totally natural, and not an attempt to be clever or funny, is shown by the fact that it happens in situations where the participants are totally wrapped up in what they are doing, and not consciously paying attention to their speech. Rugby football is a game in which emotions run high, and the surrounding crowd is continually yelling encouragement or abuse, in an inextricable mixture of English and Tok Pisin. *Come on, boys! Autim!* 'Pass it out!' *Em nau!* 'That's it!' *Some more of that! Some more, Brothers!* (Brothers is the name of a football team.) *Maski namba tu!* 'Don't pay any attention to number two!' *Good work, Jumbo. Gerim low!* 'Get him low' (English words with Tok Pisin pronunciation of [r] for [t] as in *wara* 'water'.) *Don't let them put a try! Ah, em i putim trai!* 'Ah, he scored a try.'

The examples of decreolization discussed show the way the process occurs. Phrases from the base language are borrowed in particular situations, usually where there is a strong overlap between the creole and the base language, and/or where the creole is lacking or cumbersome. The borrowed words and phrases, though seemingly isolated and innocuous, tend to have a more pernicious and far-reaching effect than is obvious at first sight. The base language spreads in all directions, like an octopus entwining its tentacles round all parts of an animal before it eventually kills it.

Language murder

Language murder is more dramatic than language suicide. The old language is slaughtered by the new. How does this happen?

The first stage is likely to be the growth of a generation of speakers who in childhood were equally skilled in two languages, both the old one which they learnt from their parents, and a new socially prestigious one to which they were exposed outside the home. As these children grow up and become adults, they gradually stop talking the older language, perhaps practising it only when they visit elderly relatives. In the course of time, they begin to forget their mother tongue. They can still converse, after a fashion, but they forget the words for things, get endings wrong, and use a limited number of sentence patterns. This phenomenon is reported fairly frequently in the literature. A typical example is Bloomfield's description of the speech of White Thunder, one of the last remaining speakers of the American Indian language Menomini: 'His Menomini is atrocious. His vocabulary is small; his inflections are often barbarous; he constructs sentences on a few threadbare models'.[8]

At the moment, we know relatively little about the detailed stages of such breakdowns, since we do not yet have enough step-by-step accounts of different language deaths. We do not know whether all languages disintegrate in the same manner, or whether different languages fall apart in different ways. One of the few detailed studies of this phenomenon is by Nancy Dorian, an American linguist who is studying the demise of Scottish Gaelic, which is a receding language throughout all of Highland Scotland.[9]

Dorian has looked in particular at isolated pockets of Gaelic speakers in three fishing villages, Brora, Golspie and Embo. These villages are situated on the eastern coast in the far north of Scotland, an area in which Gaelic has practically died out apart from the villages under discussion. In Brora and Golspie there are a number of seventy-to eighty-years-olds who were taught Gaelic as their first language, and in Embo, a more isolated village, it is possible to find people in their early forties who regard Gaelic as their mother tongue. These residual Gaelic speakers are bilingual, and a number of them speak English better than Gaelic. Most of them are aware that their Gaelic is inferior to that spoken by their parents and grandparents, and are particularly conscious of gaps in their vocabulary, explaining that their elders had many more 'words for things' than they have themselves.

Dorian divided her informants into three groups depending on their age and level of competence: older fluent speakers, younger fluent speakers and semi-speakers – the latter being those who could make themselves understood, but whose Gaelic was aberrant in a number of ways. She then compared the speech of these groups.

Superficially, one would predict a straightforward reduction in complexity in the speech of the least competent Gaelic speakers and in some constructions this was what Dorian found. For example, Gaelic has two types of passive construction (roughly comparable to sentences such as *Augustus was kicked by a cow* and *Augustus got himself kicked by a cow*). Dorian found that younger Gaelic speakers tended to confuse the two types, with one type gradually winning out over the other as a model for all passives. In the case of one mother and son pair, Dorian recorded eight correct and two incorrect attempts at translating English passives into Gaelic by the mother, a woman in her seventies. The son, on the other hand, an unmarried man in his forties who lived in his mother's household, made twelve incorrect attempts, and only one correct one.

However, in other respects the situation was more complex, as was shown when Dorian considered noun plurals. In general, the less competent speakers chose one of two paths when they could not remember the correct Gaelic inflection for a word. Sometimes they simply omitted the problem ending. At other times they retained and expanded Gaelic forms which had English equivalents, while decreasing the use of forms which were special to Gaelic, as the following paragraphs show.

There are eleven different ways of forming the plural in the East Sutherland variety of Gaelic under discussion. The four basic devices are suffixation (adding on a suffix), vowel alternation (changing the vowel), final mutation (changing the final consonant), final lengthening (lengthening the final consonant):

Type	Singular	Plural		English equivalent form
Suffixation	[preːg]	[preːgən]	'lies'	ox/oxen
Vowel alternation	[makh]	[mikh]	'sons'	foot/feet
Final mutation	[phūːnth]	[phūːntʃh]	'pounds'	_____
Final lengthening	[inʹan]	[inʹanː]	'onions'	_____

The other seven ways are basically combinations of these four. For example, [seːx] [seːçɛn] 'dishes' involves both suffixation and final mutation, and [yax] [yəiçu] 'horses' uses suffixation, vowel alternation and final mutation.

If we leave aside the mixed plurals, and look only at the simple devices, we find the following percentages of use among the three groups of speakers:

	Older fluent speakers	Younger fluent speakers	Semi- speakers
	%	%	%
Suffixation	50	44	63.5
Vowel alternation	5	4.5	4
Final mutation	10	9	5
Final lengthening	7	5.5	1
Zero	–	0.5	9

These morphological alterations were accompanied by phonological ones: Gaelic sounds not shared by English, such as [ç] (palatal fricative) tended to disappear, or were used only sporadically.

The figures quoted above show the messiness of language death. Although general trends can be discerned, the old language does not fade away neatly. Dorian noted that even in the language of the two weakest Gaelic speakers whom she interviewed, devices other than suffixation occurred in a number of plurals. Isolated words retain their Gaelic inflections right up to the end.

In the next stage, the younger generation will recognize only a few scattered Gaelic words, usually plants, foods, or town names. At this stage, the language can be said to have ·died, or, more appropriately, to have been murdered by the influx of another socially and politically dominant language.

Dorian looked at the *structural* changes involved in the collapse of Gaelic. Another linguist, Norman Denison, has examined language death in a trilingual community from a *functional* viewpoint – the uses to which the dying language is put.[10] He notes that the inhabitants of the small village of Sauris in north-east Italy were once German-speakers. Nowadays, the 800 or so villagers use three languages, Italian, Friulian, and German. Italian is the official language, used in church and school. Friulian is the local dialect, which is used in bars and for everyday conversation around the village. German, once the main language, is now gradually being ousted by the other two. In the course of the twentieth century it has gradually retreated, and become used in fewer and fewer circumstances. In recent years, it has been spoken almost exclusively in the home, as the language of intimacy between family members. Now even this function is dying out, as many parents feel that it is better for their children's future to converse with them in Italian, and German-speaking families have even begun to meet with some criticism: 'Poor child, he doesn't even speak Friulian,'[11] was a remark made by the mayor's mother about a child whose family still addressed it in German. From this viewpoint, languages simply die out because there is no need for them. As Denison notes: 'Languages at the lower end of the prestige scale retreat . . . until there is nothing left for them appropriately to be used about.'[12]

Summary

When a language dies, it does not simply fade away due to old age. Sometimes, death comes to a young language. In all cases, the extinction is due to the supplanting of the old by a new language with social and political prestige.

The death occurs either by suicide or by murder. Suicide occurs when the old and the new languages are similar. Murder occurs when they are dissimilar. Note, however, that there is not always a clear-cut line between the two types of death.

In language suicide, the language with less prestige borrows massively from the more socially acceptable one, and ends up obliterating itself. Borrowing in these circumstances is in all respects similar to other types of borrowing. It occurs first in cases where the likenesses between the borrower and donor languages are strongest, and/or where the borrower is cumbersome and lacks adequate terminology. When this type of borrowing occurs between a base language and a creole, the process is known as decreolization.

In language murder, a socially prestigious language gets used in more and more circumstances, so that previously bilingual speakers have little opportunity to practise the old language. Younger speakers tend to forget its forms and constructions, either omitting crucial endings, or utilizing those that coincide with forms found in the new language.

In brief, language death is a social phenomenon, and triggered by social needs. There is no evidence that there was anything wrong with the dead language itself: its essential structure was no better and no worse than that of any other language. It faded away because it did not fulfil the social needs of the community who spoke it.

14 *Progress or Decay?*

Assessing the situation

If you can look into the seeds of time,
And say which grain will grow and which will not....
William Shakespeare, *Macbeth*

Predicting the future depends on understanding the present. The majority of those whose opinion was quoted in Chapter 1 on the direction in which languages are moving had not considered the complexity of the factors involved in language change. They were giving rise to a purely emotional expression of their hopes and fears.

A closer look at language change has indicated that it is natural, inevitable and continuous, and involves interwoven sociolinguistic and psycholinguistic factors which cannot easily be disentangled from one another. It is triggered by social factors, but these social factors make use of existing cracks and gaps in the language structure. In the circumstances, the true direction of a change is not obvious to a superficial observer. Sometimes alterations are disruptive, as with the increasing loss of *t* in British English, where the utilization of a natural tendency to alter or omit final consonants may end up destroying a previously stable stop system. At other times, modifications can be viewed as therapy, as in the loss of *h* in British English, which is wiping out an exception in the otherwise symmetrical organization of fricatives.

However, whether changes disrupt the language system, or repair it, the most important point is this: it is in no sense wrong for human language to change, any more than it is wrong for humpback whales to alter their songs every year.[1] In fact, there are some surprising parallels between the two species. All the whales sing the same song one year, the next year they all sing a new one. But the yearly differences are not random. The songs seem to be evolving. The songs of consecutive years are more alike than those that are separated by several years. When it was first discovered that the songs of humpbacks changed from year to year, a simple explanation seemed likely. Since the whales only sing during the breeding season, and since their song is complex, it was assumed that they simply forgot the song between seasons, and then tried to reconstruct it the next year from fragments which remained in their memory. But when researchers organized a long-term study of humpbacks off the island of Maui in Hawaii, they got a surprise. The song that the whales were singing at the beginning of the new breeding season turned out to be identical to the one used at the end of the previous one. Between breeding seasons, the song had seemingly been kept in cold storage, without change. The songs were gradually modified as the season proceeded. For example, new sequences were sometimes created by joining the beginning and end of consecutive phrases, and omitting the middle part – a procedure not unlike certain human language changes.

Both whales and humans, then, are constantly changing their communication system, and are the only two species in which this has been proved to happen – though some birds are now thought to alter their song in certain ways. Rather than castigating one of these species for allowing change to occur, it seems best to admit that humans are probably programmed by nature to behave in this way. As a character in John Wyndham's novel *Web* says: 'Man is a product of nature . . . . Whatever he does, it must be part of his nature to do – or he could not do it. He is not, and cannot be *un*natural. He, with his capacities, is as much the product of nature as were the dinosaurs with theirs. He is an *instrument* of natural processes.'

A consideration of the naturalness and inevitability of change leads us to the three final questions which need to be discussed in this book. First, is it still relevant to speak of progress or decay? Secondly, irrespective of whether the move is a forwards or backwards one, are human languages evolving in any detectable direction? Thirdly, even though language change is not wrong in the moral sense, is it socially undesirable, and, if so, can we control it?

Let us consider these matters.

Forwards or backwards?

'Once, twice, thrice upon a time, there lived a jungle. This particular jungle started at the bottom and went upwards till it reached the monkeys, who had been waiting years for the trees to reach them, and as soôn as they did, the monkeys invented climbing down.' The opening paragraph of Spike Milligan's fable, *The Story of the Bald Twit Lion*, indicates how easy it is to make facts fit one's preferred theory.

This tendency is particularly apparent in past interpretations of the direction of change, where opinions about progress or decay in language have tended to reflect the religious or philosophical preconceptions of their proponents, rather than a detached analysis of the evidence. Let us briefly deal with these preconceptions before looking at the issue itself.

Many nineteenth-century scholars were imbued with sentimental ideas about the 'noble savage', and assumed that the current generation was by comparison a race of decadent sinners. They therefore took it for granted that language had declined from a former state of perfection. Restoring this early perfection was viewed as one of the principal goals of comparative historical linguistics: 'A principal goal of this science is to reconstruct the full, pure forms of an original stage from the variously disfigured and mutilated forms which are attested in the individual languages,' said one scholar.[2]

This quasi-religious conviction of gradual decline has never entirely died out. But from the mid-nineteenth century onward, a second, opposing viewpoint came into existence alongside the earlier one. Darwin's doctrine of the survival of the fittest and ensuing belief in inevitable progress gradually grew in popularity: 'Progress, therefore, is not an accident, but a necessity. . . . It is a part of nature,'[3] claimed one nineteenth-century enthusiast. Darwin himself believed that in language 'the better, the shorter, the easier forms are constantly gaining the upper hand, and they owe their success to their inherent virtue,'[4]

The doctrine of the survival of the fittest, in its crudest version, implies that those forms and languages which survive are inevitably better than those which die out. This is unfortunate, since it confuses the notions of progress and decay in language with expansion and decline. As we have seen, expansion and decline reflect political and social situations, not the intrinsic merit or decadence of a language. For example, it is a historical accident that English is so widely spoken in the world. Throughout history, quite different types of language – Latin, Turkish, Chinese, for example – have spread over wide areas. This popularity reflects the military and political strength of these nations, not the worth of their speech. Similarly, Gaelic is dying out because it is being ousted by English, a language with social and political prestige. It is not collapsing because it has got too complicated or strange for people to speak, as has occasionally been maintained.

In order to assess the possible direction of language, then, we need to put aside both religious beliefs and Darwinian assumptions. The former leads to an illogical idealization of the past, and the latter to the confusion of progress and decay with expansion and decline.

Leaving aside these false trails, we are left with a crucial question: what might we mean by 'progress' within language?

The term 'progress' implies a movement towards some desired endpoint. What could this be, in terms of linguistic excellence? A number of linguists are in no doubt. They endorse the view of Jespersen, who maintained that 'that language ranks highest which goes farthest in the art of accomplishing much with little means, or, in other words, which is able to express the greatest amount of meaning with the simplest mechanism.'[5]

If this criterion were taken seriously, we would be obliged to rank pidgins as the most advanced languages. As we have already noted (Chapter 12), true simplicity seems to be counterbalanced by ambiguity and cumbersomeness. Darwin's confident belief in the 'inherent virtue' of shorter and easier forms must be set beside the realization that such forms often result in confusing homonyms, as in the Tok Pisin *hat* for 'hot', 'hard', 'hat', and 'heart'.

A straightforward simplicity measure then will not necessarily pinpoint the 'best' language. A considerable number of other factors must be taken into account, and it is not yet clear which they are, and how they should be assessed. In brief, linguists have been unable to decide on any clear measure of excellence, even though the majority are of the opinion that a language with numerous irregularities should be less highly ranked than one which is economical and transparent. Note, however, that preliminary attempts to rank languages in this way have run into a further problem.

A language which is simple and regular in one respect is likely to be complex and confusing in others. There seems to be a trading relationship between the different parts of the grammar which we do not fully understand. This has come out clearly in the work of one researcher who has compared the progess of Turkish and Yugoslav children as they acquired their respective languages.[6] Turkish children find it exceptionally easy to learn the inflections of their language, which are remarkably straightforward, and they master the entire system by the age of two. But the youngsters struggle with relative clauses (the equivalent of English clauses beginning with *who*, *which*, *that*) until around the age of five. Yugoslav children, on the other hand, have great problems with the inflectional system of Serbo-Croatian, which is 'a classic Indo-European synthetic muddle', and they are not competent at manipulating it until around the age of five. Yet, they have no problems with Serbo-Croatian relative clauses, which they can normally cope with by the age of two.

Overall, we cannot yet specify satisfactorily just what we mean by a 'perfect' language, except in a very broad sense. The most we can do is to note that a certain part of one language may be simpler and therefore perhaps 'better' than that of another.

Meanwhile, even if all agreed that a perfectly regular language was the 'best', there is no evidence that languages are progressing towards this ultimate goal. Instead, there is a continuous pull betweeen the disruption and restoration of patterns. In this perpetual ebb and flow, it would be a mistake to regard pattern neatening and regularization as a step forwards. Such an occurrence may be no more progressive than the tidying up of a cluttered office. Reorganization simply restores the room to a workable state. Similarly, it would be misleading to assume that pattern disruption was necessarily a backward step. Structural dislocation may be the result of extending the language in some useful way.

We must conclude therefore that language is ebbing and flowing like the tide, but neither progressing nor decaying, as far as we can tell. Disruptive and therapeutic tendencies vie with one another, with neither one totally winning or losing, resulting in a perpetual stalemate. As the famous Russian linguist Roman Jakobson said fifty years ago: 'The spirit of equilibrium and the simultaneous tendency towards its rupture constitute the indispensable properties of that whole that is language.'[7]

Are languages evolving?

Leaving aside notions of progress and decay we need to ask one further question. Is there any evidence that languages as a whole are moving in any particular direction in their intrinsic structure? Are they, for example, moving towards a fixed word order, as has sometimes been claimed?

It is clear that languages, even if they are evolving in some identifiable way, are doing so very slowly – otherwise all languages would be rather more similar than they in fact are. However, unfortunately for those who would like to identify some overall drift, the languages of the world seem to be moving in different, often opposite, directions.

For example, over the past two thousand years or so, most Indo-European languages have moved from being SOV (subject-object-verb) languages, to SVO (subject-verb-object) ones. As we noted in Chapter 7, certain Niger-Congo languages seem to be following a similar path. Yet we cannot regard this as an overall trend, since Mandarin Chinese seems to be undergoing a change in the opposite direction, from SVO to SOV.[8]

During the same period, English and a number of other Indo-European languages have gradually lost their inflections, and moved over to a fixed word order. However, this direction is not inevitable, since Wappo, a Californian Indian language, appears to be doing the reverse, and moving from a system in which grammatical relationships are expressed by word order to one in which they are marked by case endings.[9]

A similar variety is seen in the realm of phonology. For example, English, French and Hindi had the same common ancestor: nowadays, Hindi has sixteen stop consonants and ten vowels, according to one count. French, on the other hand, has sixteen vowels and six stops. English, meanwhile, has acquired more fricatives than either of these two languages, some of which speakers of

French and Hindi find exceptionally difficult to pronounce. Many more such examples could be found.

Overall, then we must conclude that 'the evolution of
language as such has never been demonstrated, and the
inherent equality of all languages must be maintained on
present evidence.'[10]

Is language change socially undesirable?

Let us now turn to the last two questions. Is language
change undesirable? If so, is it controllable?

Social undesirability and moral turpitude are often
confused. Yet the two questions can quite often be kept
distinct. For example, it is certainly not 'wrong' to sleep
out in the open. Nevertheless, it is fairly socially inconvenient to have people bedding down wherever they want
to, and therefore laws have been passed forbidding people to camp out in, say, Trafalgar Square or Hyde Park in
London.

Language change is, we have seen, in no sense wrong.
But is it socially undesirable? It is only undesirable when
communication gets disrupted. If different groups change
a previously unified language in different directions, or if
one group alters its speech more radically than another,
mutual intelligibility may be impaired or even destroyed.
In Tok Pisin, for example, speakers from rural areas have
great difficulty in understanding the urbanized varieties.
This is an unhappy and socially inconvenient state of
affairs.

In England, on the other hand, the problem is minimal.
There are relatively few speakers of British English who
cannot understand one another. This is because most
people speak the same basic dialect, in the sense that the
rules underlying their utterances and vocabulary are fairly
much the same. They are likely, however, to speak this
single dialect with different accents. There is nothing

wrong with this, as long as people can communicate satisfactorily with one another. An accent which differs markedly from those around may be hard for others to comprehend, and is therefore likely to be a disadvantage in job-hunting situations, as a number of recent immigrants have found. But a mild degree of regional variation is probably a mark of individuality to be encouraged rather than stamped out.

A number of people censure the variety of regional accents in England, maintaining that the accent that was originally of one particular area, London and the southeast, is 'better' than the others. In fact, speakers from this locality sometimes claim that they speak English *without* an accent, something which is actually impossible. It is, of course, currently socially useful in England to be able to speak the accent of so-called Southern British English, an accent sometimes spoken of as Received Pronunciation (RP), which has spread to the educated classes throughout the country. But there is no logical reason behind the disapproval of regional accents. Moreover, such objections are by no means universal. In America, a regional accent is simply a mark of where you are from with no stigma attached, for the most part.

Accent differences, then, are not a matter of great concern. More worrying are instances where differing dialects cause unintelligibility, or misunderstandings. In the past, this often used to be the case in England. Caxton, writing in the fifteenth century, notes that 'comyn englysshe that is spoken in one shyre varyeth from another'.[11] To illustrate his point, he narrates an episode concerning a ship which was stranded in the Thames for lack of wind, and put into shore for refreshment. One of the merchants on board went to a nearby house, and asked, in English, for meat and eggs. The lady of the house, much to this gentleman's indignation, replied that she could not speak French! In Caxton's words, the merchant 'cam in to an hows and axed for mete and specyally he axyd after eggys. And the good wyf answerde that she coude speke no frenshe. And the merchaunt was angry for he also coude speke no frenshe, but wolde haue hadde egges and she vnderstode hym not.' The problem in this case was that a 'new' Norse word *egges* 'eggs' was in the process of replacing the Old English word *eyren*, but was not yet generally understood.

Unfortunately, such misunderstandings did not disappear with the fifteenth century. Even though, both in America and England, the majority of speakers are mutually intelligible, worrying misunderstandings still occur through dialect differences. Consider the conversation between Samuel, a five-year-old coloured boy from West Philadelphia, and Paul, a white psychologist who had been working in Samuel's school for six months:

Samuel: I been know your name.
Paul: What?
Samuel: I been know your name.
Paul: You better know my name?
Samuel: I *been* know your name.[12]

Paul failed to realize that in Philadelphia's black community *been* means 'for a long time'. Samuel meant 'I have known your name for a long time.' In some circumstances, this use of *been* can be completely misleading to a white speaker. A coloured Philadelphian who said *I been married* would in fact mean 'I have been married for a long time.' But a white speaker would normally interpret her sentence as meaning 'I have been married, but I am not married any longer.'

Is it possible to do anything about situations where differences caused by language change threaten to disrupt the mutual comprehension and cohesion of a population? Should language change be stopped?

If legislators decide that something is socially inconvenient, then their next task is to decide whether it is possible to take effective action against it. If we attempted to halt language change by law, would the result be as effective as forbidding people to camp in Trafalgar Square? Or would it be as useless as telling the pigeons there not to roost around the fountains? Judging by the experience of the French who have an academy, the Académie Française, which adjudicates over matters of linguistic usage, and whose findings have been made law in some cases, the result is a waste of time. Even though there may be some limited effect on the written language, spoken French appears not to have responded in any noticeable way.

If legal sanctions are impractical, how can mutual comprehension be brought about or maintained? The answer is not to attempt to limit change, which is probably impossible, but to ensure that all members of the population have at least one common language, and one common variety of that language, which they can mutually use. The standard language may be the only one spoken by certain people. Others will retain their own regional dialect or language alongside the standard one. This is the situation in the British Isles, where some Londoners, for example, speak only standard British English. In Wales, however, there are a number of people who are equally fluent in Welsh and English.

The imposition of a standard language cannot be brought about by force. Sometimes it occurs spontaneously, as has happened in England. At other times, conscious intervention is required. Such social planning requires tact and skill. In order for a policy to achieve acceptance, a population must *want* to speak a particular language or particular variety of it. A branch of sociolinguistics known as 'language planning' or, more recently, 'language engineering' is attempting to solve the practical and theoretical problems involved in such attempts.[13]

Once standardization has occurred, and a whole population has accepted one particular variety as standard, it becomes a strong unifying force and often a source of national pride and symbol of independence.

Great Permitters

Perhaps we need one final comment about 'Great Permitters' – a term coined by William Safire, who writes a column about language for the *New York Times*.[14] These are intelligent, determined people, often writers, who 'care about clarity and precision, who detest fuzziness of expression that reveals sloppiness or laziness of thought'. They want to give any changes which occur 'a shove in the direction of freshness and precision', and are 'willing to struggle to preserve the clarity and color in the language'. In other words, they are prepared to accept new usages which they regard as advantageous, and are prepared to battle against those which seem sloppy or pointless.

Such an aim is admirable. An influential writer-journalist can clearly make interesting suggestions, and provide models for others to follow. Two points need to be made, however. First, however hard a 'linguistic activist' (as Safire calls himself) works, he is unlikely to reverse a strong trend, however much he would like to. Safire has, for example, given up his fight against *hopefully*, and also against *viable* which, he regretfully admits, 'cannot be killed'. Secondly, and perhaps more importantly, we need to realize how personal and how idiosyncratic are judgments as to what is 'good' and what is 'bad', even when they are made by a careful and knowledgeable writer, as becomes clear from the often furious letters which follow Safire's pronouncements in the *New York Times*. Even a Safire fan must admit that he holds a number of opinions which are based on nothing more than a subjective feeling about the words in question. Why, for example, did he give up the struggle against *hopefully*, but continue to wage war on *clearly*? As one of his correspondents notes, 'Your grudge against clearly is unclear to me.' Similarly, Safire attacks ex-President Carter's 'needless substitution of encrypt for encode', but is sharply reminded by a reader that 'the words "encrypt" and "encode" have very distinct meanings for a cryptographer.' These, and other similar examples, show that attempts of caring persons to look after a language can mean no more than the preservation of personal preferences which may not agree with the views of others.

Summary and conclusion

Continual language change is natural and inevitable, and is due to a combination of psycholinguistic and sociolinguistic factors.

Once we have stripped away religious and philosophical preconceptions, there is no evidence that language is either progressing or decaying. Disruption and therapy seem to balance one another in a perpetual stalemate. These two opposing pulls are an essential characteristic of language.

Furthermore, there is no evidence that languages are moving in any particular direction from the point of view of language structure – several are moving in contrary directions.

Language change is in no sense wrong, but it may, in certain circumstances, be socially undesirable. Minor variations in pronunciation from region to region are unimportant, but change which disrupts the mutual intelligibility of a community can be socially and politically inconvenient. If this happens, it may be useful to encourage standardization – the adoption of a standard variety of one particular language which everybody will be able to use, alongside the existing regional dialects or languages. Such a situation must be brought about gradually, with tact and care, since a population will only adopt a language or dialect it *wants* to speak.

Finally, it is always possible that language is developing in some mysterious fashion that linguists have not yet identified. Only time and further research will tell. There is much more to be discovered.

But we may finish on a note of optimism. We no longer, like Caxton in the fifteenth century, attribute language change to the domination of man's affairs by the moon:

And certaynly our langage now vsed varyeth ferre from that which was vsed and spoken whan I was borne. For we englysshe men ben borne vnder the domynacyon of the mone, which is neuer stedfaste but euer wauerynge wexynge one season and waneth and dycreaseth another season.[15]

Instead, step by step, we are coming to an understanding of the social and psychological factors underlying language change. As the years go by, we hope gradually to increase this knowledge. In the words of the nineteenth-century poet, Alfred Lord Tennyson:

Science moves, but slowly slowly, creeping on from point to point.

Symbols and Terminology

Most symbols and terms are explained in the text the first time they occur. But since several common ones occur more than once, this glossary has been added for the benefit of those readers not familiar with them.

General

[ ] Square brackets indicate sounds. For example, the pronunciation of the English word *kissed* may be represented by the phonetic transcription [kɪst].

* An asterisk indicates a non-permitted sequence of sounds or words in the language concerned. For example, English does not permit a word with the sound sequence *[tpet], or a sentence *Augusta roses wants.

→ An arrow means 'changed into historically', as in [e] → [i], which means [e] changed into [i].

Consonants

[θ] The sound at the beginning of English *thick*.
[ð] The sound at the beginning of *then*.
[ʃ] The sound at the beginning of *shock*.
[ʒ] The sound at the end of *beige* or in the middle of *leisure*
[tʃ] The sound at the beginning and end of *church*.
[dʒ] The sound at the beginning and ending of *judge*.
[ŋ] The sound at the end of *bang* (**velar nasal**).
[ʔ] A **glottal stop** – see explanation overleaf.

Stop. A consonant involving a complete stoppage of the airstream at some point in the vocal tract, as [p], [t], [k]. A glottal stop [ʔ] is a complete stoppage of the airstream in the glottis (lower part of the throat), as at the end of Cockney or Glaswegian *pit* [pɪʔ], or between words in German.

Fricative. A consonant in which the airstream is never completely cut off, resulting in audible friction, as in [f], [v], [s], [z].

Voiced. A voiced sound is one whose production involves vibration of the vocal cords, as in [b], [d], [g], [v], [z].

Voiceless. A voiceless sound is one whose production does not involve the vibration of the vocal cords as in [p], [t], [k], [f], [s].

Vowels

: A colon added to a vowel indicates length, as in [ti:] *tea*. ˜ A wavy line over a vowel indicates nasalization, as in French [bɔ̃] *bon* 'good'.

[ə] **Schwa**, a short indeterminate vowel, like that at the beginning of *ago*, or the end of *sofa*.

[i:] A vowel somewhat like that in *meet, bee*. (Other vowel symbols are explained as they occur. Key words are less useful for vowels, since there is so much variation in accent in the English speaking world.)

Diphthong. A sequence of two vowels which glide into one another, as in *play* [pleɪ].

Notes

Further details of books and articles referred to are given in the Select Bibliography.

Chapter 1 The Ever-whirling Wheel

1 In Lehmann, 1967:63.
2 In Fisher & Bornstein, 1974:77.
3 *Troylus and Criseyde* II, 22–6.
4 Saussure, 1915/1959:77.
5 Spike Hughes, *Daily Telegraph*, 26 April 1968.
6 Anthony Lejeune, *Daily Telegraph*, 7 May 1971.
7 Mary Stott, *Guardian*, 9 September 1968.
8 Douglas Bush, *American Scholar*, Spring 1972:244.
9 David Holloway, *Daily Telegraph*, 7 July 1978.
10 Richard Gilman, *Decadence*, London: Secker & Warburg, 1979.
11 Philip Howard, *Words Fail Me*, London: Hamish Hamilton, 1980.
12 Anthony Lejeune, *Daily Telegraph*, 7 May 1971.
13 In Jespersen, 1922:322.
14 Jespersen, 1922:263
15 Vendryès, 1925:359.
16 In Hyman, 1975:131.
17 In Wilkinson, 1967:18–19.
18 In Jespersen, 1922:42.
19 In Pyles, 1971:225.
20 Lowth, 1762/1967:i, ix.
21 Sapir, 1921:124.
22 *The Rambler*, 15 January 1752.
23 Pyles, 1971:224.
24 Lowth, 1762/1967:127–8.

25 *Canterbury Tales, Prologue*, 70–73.
26 John Wallis, in Jespersen, 1942:II, 161.
27 Lowth, 1762:x.
28 See Aitchison, 1978; Lyons, 1981; Smith &' Wilson, 1979, for brief introductions to linguistics.
29 Lakoff, 1975:28.

Chapter 2 Collecting up Clues

1 J. Kuper (ed.), *The Anthropologist's Cookbook*, London: Routledge & Kegan Paul, 1977.
2 Saussure, 1915/1959:51.
3 Conan Doyle, *A Case of Identity*.
4 *A Midsummer Night's Dream*, II, ii, 9–12.
5 *Twelfth Night*, I, iii, 97f.
6 *The Merchant of Venice*, IV, i, 123–4.
7 Cicero, *Div* ii, 84, in Allen, 1978:98.
8 Allen, 1975:67.
9 Catullus, 84.
10 *Pickwick Papers*, ch. 34.
11 Allen, 1978:34.
12 John Hart, in Danielsson, 1955:190.
13 'F litteram imum labrum superis imprimentes dentibus, reflexa ad palati fastigium lingua, leni spiramine proferemus.' Mar. Vict, κ vi, 34, partially quoted in Allen, 1978:34.
14 Chomsky & Halle, 1968:249f.
15 Jespersen, 1942:I, 201.

Chapter 3 Charting the Changes

1 Bloomfield, 1933:347.
2 Hockett, 1958:439.
3 Saussure, 1915/1959:17.
4 Saussure, 1915/1959:125.
5 Joos, 1961.
6 Lakoff, 1975:26.
7 Sapir, 1921:38.

8 Hubbell, 1950:48.
9 Labov, 1972:43.
10 Labov, 1972:47.
11 Labov, 1972:70f.
12 Labov, 1972:93.
13 Labov, 1972:94.
14 Labov, 1972:90.
15 Labov, 1972:89.
16 Labov, 1972:92.
17 Labov, 1972:91.
18 Labov, 1972:114.

Chapter 4 Spreading the Word

1 Sturtevant, 1917/1961:82.
2 Labov, 1972:123.
3 Labov, 1972:132.
4 Labov, 1972:136.
5 Hubbell, 1950:48.
6 From Labov, 1972:114.
7 Labov, 1972:115.
8 Labov, 1972:24.
9 Labov, 1972:141.
10 Labov, 1972:145.
11 Sturtevant, 1917/1961:26.
12 Sturtevant, 1917/1961:77.
13 Labov, 1972:317.
14 Milroy & Milroy, 1978; Milroy, 1980.
15 Labov, 1972:1f.
16 Labov, 1972:28.
17 Labov, 1972:29.
18 Labov, 1972:32.

Chapter 5 Conflicting Loyalties

1 Labov, 1972:226.
2 *The Oxford Dictionary of Nursery Rhymes*, I.Opie &
   P.Opie (eds.), Oxford: Clarendon Press, 1951:294.
3 A.A. Wood, in Trudgill, 1974:9.

4 Trudgill, 1974.
5 In Pyles, 1971:191.
6 Diagram constructed from table in Trudgill, 1974:94.
7 Trudgill, 1972; 1974:94.
8 Labov, 1972a:65.
9 Cheshire, 1978.

Chapter 6 Catching on and Taking off

1 Sapir, 1921:178.
2 Osthoff & Brugmann (1878). Translation (slightly different from mine) in Lehmann, 1967:204.
3 Meillet, quoted by Vendryès, in Keiler, 1972:109.
4 Labov, 1972:148.
5 Labov, 1972:20.
6 Hooper, 1976a; 1978.
7 Fidelholtz, 1975.
8 Cheshire, 1978:59.
9 Krishnamurti, 1978.
10 Labov, 1972:19.
11 Cheshire, 1978:59.
12 Fidelholtz, 1975:208.
13 Wang, 1969; Chen, 1972.
14 Sommerfelt, in Chen, 1972.
15 Chen & Wang, 1975.
16 Chen, 1972:47.
17 Chen & Wang, 1975:276; Chen, 1976:215.
18 Chen, 1972:474.
19 Lightfoot, 1979; Aitchison, 1980.
20 *Othello*, III, iii, 177.
21 *Hamlet*, III, iii, 19.
22 Potter, 1969.
23 *Antony and Cleopatra*, IV, xiii, 18.
24 *Antony and Cleopatra* IV, xii, 50.
25 *Hamlet*, II, ii, 193.
26 Potter, 1969:121.
27 *Measure for Measure*, III, ii, 241.
28 Potter, 1969:121.
29 Martinet, 1955:36.

Chapter 7 The Reason Why

1 Ohala, 1974:269.
2 H. Collitz, in Jespersen, 1922:257.
3 Jespersen, 1922:257.
4 Bloomfield, 1933:385.
5 King, 1969:189.
6 Harris, 1969:550.
7 Postal, 1968:283.
8 Hockett, 1958:440.
9 Hockett, 1958:441.
10 Hockett, 1958:443–5.
11 Labov, 1972:171.
12 Gumperz & Wilson, 1971.
13 Bynon, 1977:244.
14 Koch, 1974:104.
15 David Bonavia, *The Times*, 21 June 1971.
16 Whitely, in Bynon, 1977:231.
17 Deirdre Wilson, unpublished research notes on French dialects.
18 Bickerton, 1973:644.
19 Bickerton, 1973.
20 Laurie Colwin, *Happy All the Time*, London: Chatto & Windus, 1979.
21 C. Sandberg in *The Treasury of Humorous Quotations*, London: Dent, 1962.
22 Baron, 1974.
23 Labov, 1972:234.
24 Lass, 1980.

Chapter 8 Doing What Comes Naturally

1 Quoted by Macdonald Critchley in Goodglass & Blumstein, 1973:64.
2 Stampe, 1969; 1979.
3 Hooper, 1976:85.
4 Hooper, 1976:106.
5 Chen & Wang, 1975.
6 Chen & Wang, 1975.

7 O'Connor, 1973:251.
8 Ohala, 1974a.
9 Ohala, 1974.
10 Hombert, Ohala & Ewan, 1979.
11 Janson, in Chen & Wang, 1975.
12 Twaddell, 1935.
13 Martinet, 1960/1964:214; Akamatsu, 1967.
14 Hyman, 1975; Pullum, 1977.
15 Smith & Wilson, 1979:48.
16 Aitchison, 1979.
17 Hyman, 1975.
18 Harris, 1978.
19 Hale, 1973.

Chapter 9 Repairing the Patterns

1 Elcock, 1960.
2 Jespersen, 1942.
3 Jespersen, 1942.
4 Lightfoot, 1979.
5 Kiparsky, 1968; King, 1969.

Chapter 10 The Mad Hatter's Tea-party

1 Prokosch, 1938.
2 Chomsky & Halle, 1968.
3 Martinet, 1955.
4 King, 1969:195; Bynon, 1977:174.
5 Chen, 1976:232.
6 Herzog, in King, 1969:197.
7 King, 1969; 1969a.
8 Chen, 1976:220.
9 Lass, 1976.
10 Greenberg, 1963; Lehmann, 1973.
11 Kuno, 1974; Vincent, 1976.
12 Aitchison, 1979.
13 Li & Thompson, 1974; Vincent 1976; Aitchison, 1979.

Chapter 11 Development and Breakdown

1 Jespersen, 1922:421, 434.
2 King, 1969:80.
3 Paul, Whitney, Passy quoted in King, 1969:78.
4 Sweet, in Jespersen, 1922:161.
5 King, 1969:65.
6 Andersen, 1978:21.
7 Akmajian, Demers & Harnish, 1979:210.
8 Halle, 1962, followed by most linguists working within a transformational-generative framework (e.g. Kiparsky, 1968; Postal, 1968; King, 1969).
9 Kiparsky, 1968:195.
10 Kiparsky, 1968:193.
11 Klima & Bellugi, 1966.
12 Lenneberg, 1967; Aitchison, 1976.
13 R. Neville & J. Clarke, *Bad Blood*, London: Jonathan Cape, 1979.
14 Smith, 1973.
15 Stampe, 1969; 1979.
16 Drachman, 1978.
17 Lester & Skousen, 1974.
18 Speech errors are from my own collection; from that of an LSE student, Elaine Simmonds; and from Fromkin, 1973.
19 Fromkin, 1973:13.
20 *New York Times*, 20 August 1971.
21 Safire, 1980:96.
22 Safire, 1980:98.
23 Gardner, 1974:61.
24 Jakobson, 1968:60.
25 Fry, 1959; Shankweiler & Harris, 1966.

Chapter 12 Language Birth

1 Jespersen, 1922:413.
2 Todd, 1974; Hancock, 1979.
3 Information on Tok Pisin from Hall, 1966; Mihalic, 1971; Dutton, 1973; Mühlhäusler, 1979; and my own recordings and observations made on a field trip to Papua New Guinea, March 1980.

4 French, in Hall, 1966:107.
5 Hall, 1966.
6 M. Bertrand-Boconde, in Meijer & Muysken, 1977:22.
7 Valdman, 1977; Naro 1978.
8 Naro, 1978.
9 Bloomfield, 1933:472.
10 Kay & Sankoff, 1974.
11 Mühlhäusler, 1978, 1979.
12 Mühlhäusler, 1978:72.
13 Mühlhäusler, 1979, 1979a.
14 Todd, 1974:4.
15 Information on creolization in Tok Pisin from Mühlhäusler, 1979; Sankoff & Laberge, 1974; Sankoff, 1977; and my own recordings and observations.

Chapter 13 Language Death

1 Bopp, 1827, in Jespersen, 1922:65.
2 Bickerton, 1971, 1973.
3 Bickerton, 1971.
4 Examples of decreolization in Tok Pisin from my own recordings and observations.
5 Mühlhäusler, 1979:151.
6 NBC radio broadcast, March 1980.
7 NBC radio advertisement, March 1980.
8 Bloomfield, 1927:395.
9 Dorian, 1973, 1978.
10 Denison, 1972, 1977.
11 Denison, 1972:68.
12 Denison, 1977:21.

Chapter 14 Progress or Decay?

1 Payne, 1979.
2 Curtius, 1871, in Kiparsky, 1972:35.
3 Herbert Spencer, *Social Statics* (1850).
4 Darwin, 1871, in Labov, 1972:273.
5 Mühlhäusler, 1979:151.

6 Slobin, 1977.
7 Jakobson, 1949:336. Translation in Keiler, 1972.
8 Li & Thompson, 1974.
9 Li & Thompson, 1976.
10 Greenberg, 1957:65:
11 Caxton, preface to *Erydos* (1490).
12 Labov, 1972a: 62
13 Bell, 1976; Wurm, Mühlhäusler & Laycock, 1977.
14 Safire, 1980, from whom the quotations in this section are taken.
15 Caxton, preface to *Erydos* (1490).

Select Bibliography

AITCHISON, J. (1976), *The Articulate Mammal*, London: Hutchinson; New York: Universe, McGraw-Hill.

AITCHISON, J. (1978), *Linguistics*, London: Hodder and Stoughton, Teach Yourself Books.

AITCHISON, J. (1979), 'The order of word order change', *Transactions of the Philological Society*, 43–65.

AITCHISON, J. (1980), Review of LIGHTFOOT (1979), *Linguistics*, 17, 137–46.

AKAMATSU, T. (1967), 'Quelques statistiques sur la fréquence d'utilisation des voyelles nasales françaises', *La Linguistique*, I, 75–80.

AKMAJIAN, A, DEMERS, R.A. and HARNISH, R.M. (1979), *Linguistics: An Introduction to Language and Communication*, Cambridge, Mass: MIT Press.

ALLEN, W.S. (1974), *Vox Graeca: A Guide to the Pronunciation of Classical Greek*, second edition, Cambridge: University Press.

ALLEN, W.S. (1978), *Vox Latina: A Guide to the Pronunciation of Classical Latin*, second edition, Cambridge: University Press.

ANDERSEN, H, (1978), 'Perceptual and conceptual factors in abductive innovations', in FISIAK (1978).

ANDERSON, J.M. and JONES, C. (eds) (1974), *Historical Linguistics*, Amsterdam: North Holland.

BACH, E. and HARMS, R.T. (eds) (1968), *Universals in Linguistic Theory*, New York: Holt, Rinehart & Winston.

BARON, N. (1974), 'Functional motivation for age grading in linguistic innovation', in ANDERSON and JONES (1974).

BELL, R. (1976), *Sociolinguistics: Goals, approaches, and problems*, London: Batsford.

BICKERTON, D. (1971), 'Inherent variability and variable rules', *Foundations of Language*, 7, 457–92.

BICKERTON, D. (1973), 'The nature of a creole continuum', *Language*, 49, 640–69.

BLOOMFIELD, L. (1933), *Language*, New York: Holt, Rinehart & Winston.

BYNON, T. (1977), *Historical Linguistics*, Cambridge: University Press.

CHEN, M. (1972), 'The time dimension: contribution toward a theory of sound change', *Foundations of Language*, 8, 457–98.

CHEN, M. (1976), 'Relative chronology: three methods of reconstruction', *Journal of Linguistics*, 12, 209–58.

CHEN, M. and WANG, W. (1975), 'Sound change: actuation and implementation', *Language*, 51, 255–81.

CHESHIRE, J. (1978), 'Present tense verbs in Reading English', in TRUDGILL (1978).

CHOMSKY, N., and HALLE, M. (1968), *The Sound Pattern of English*, New York: Harper & Row.

CHRISTIE, W. (1976), *Proceedings of the Second International Conference on Historical Linguistics*, Amsterdam: North Holland.

DANIELSSON, B. (1955), *John Hart's Works on English Orthography and Pronunciation* Part I, Stockholm: Almquist and Wiksell.

DECAMP, D. and HANCOCK, I.F. (eds) (1974), *Pidgins and Creoles: Current Trends and Prospects*, Washington, D.C.: Georgetown University Press.

DENISON, N. (1972), 'Some observations on language variety and plurilingualism', in *Sociolinguistics*, J.B. Pride and J. Holmes (eds), Harmondsworth: Penguin.

DENISON, N. (1977), 'Language death or language suicide?', *Linguistics*, 191, 13–22.

DORIAN, N. (1973), 'Grammatical change in a dying dialect', *Language*, 49, 413–38.

DORIAN, N. (1978), 'The fate of morphological complexity in language death', *Language*, 54, 590–609.

DRACHMAN, G. (1978), 'Child language and language change: a conjecture and some refutations', in FISIAK (1978).

DUTTON, T.E. (1973), *Conversational New Guinea Pidgin*, Canberra: Pacific Linguistics, D-12.

ELCOCK, W.D. (1960), *The Romance Languages*, London: Faber & Faber.

FIDELHOLTZ, J.L. (1975), 'Word frequency and vowel reduction in English', *Papers from the Eleventh Regional Meeting*, Chicago: Chicago Linguistic Society.

FISHER, J.H. and BORNSTEIN, D. (1974), *In Forme of Speche is Chaunge*, Englewood Cliffs, N.J.: Prentice-Hall.

FISIAK, J. (1978), *Recent Developments in Historical Phonology*, The Hague: Mouton.

FROMKIN, V.A. (1973), *Speech Errors as Linguistic Evidence*, The Hague: Mouton.

FRY, D.B. (1959), 'Phonemic substitutions in an aphasic patient', *Language and Speech*, 2, 52–61.

GARDNER, H. (1974), *The Shattered Mind*, New York: Random House; Vintage Books, 1976.

GIMSON, A.C. (1980), *An Introduction to the Pronunciation of English*, third edition, London: Edward Arnold.

GOODGLASS, H. and BLUMSTEIN, S. (1973), *Psycholinguistics and Aphasia*, Baltimore: John Hopkins University Press.

GREENBERG, J.H. (1957), *Essays in Linguistics*, Chicago: University Press; Phoenix Books ed, 1963.

GREENBERG, J.H. (1963), 'Some universals of grammar with particular reference to the order of meaningful elements', in *Universals of Language*, J.H. Greenberg (ed.), Cambridge, Mass: MIT Press.

GUMPERZ, J. and WILSON, R. (1971), 'Convergence and creolization: a case from the Indo-Aryan/Dravidian border', in HYMES (1971).

HALE, K. (1973), 'Deep-surface canonical disparities in relation to analysis and change: an Australian example', in *Current Trends in Linguistics*, T.A. Sebeok (ed.), vol. II. *Diachronic, Areal and Typological Linguistics*, The Hague: Mouton.

HALL, R. (1966), *Pidgin and Creole Languages*, Ithaca: Cornell University Press.

HALLE, M. (1962), 'Phonology in generative grammar', *Word*, 18, 54–72. Also in *The Structure of Language*, J.A. Fodor and J.A. Katz (eds), Englewood Cliffs, N.J.: Prentice-Hall, 1964.

HANCOCK, I.F. (1979). 'On the origins of the term *pidgin*' in *Readings in Creole Studies*, I.F. Hancock (ed.), Ghent: E. Story-Scientia.

HARRIS, J.W. (1969), 'Sound change in Spanish and the theory of markedness', *Language*, 45, 538–552.

HARRIS, M. (ed.) (1976), *Romance Syntax*, Salford: University of Salford.

HARRIS, M.B. (1978), 'The inter-relationship between phonological and grammatical change', in FISIAK (1978).

HOCKETT, C. (1958), *A Course in Modern Linguistics*, New York: Macmillan.

HOMBERT, J.M., OHALA, J. and EWAN, W., (1979) 'Phonetic explanations for the development of tones', *Language*, 55, 37–58.

HOOPER, J. (1976), *An introduction to Natural Generative Phonology*, New York: Academic Press.

HOOPER, J.B. (1976a), 'Word frequency in lexical diffusion and the source of morphophonological change', in CHRISTIE (1976).

HOOPER, J.B. (1978), 'Constraints on schwa-deletion in American English', in FISIAK (1978).

HUBBELL, A.F. (1950), *The Pronunciation of English in New York City*, New York: Columbia University Press.

HYMAN, L.M. (1975), 'On the change from SOV to SVO: evidence from Niger-Congo', in *Word Order and Word Order Change*, C.N. Li (ed.), Austin: University of Texas Press.

HYMES, D. (ed.) (1971), *Pidginization and Creolization of Languages*, Cambridge: University Press.

JAKOBSON, R. (1968), *Child Language, Aphasia and Phonological Universals*, The Hague: Mouton. Original Title *Kindersprache, Aphasie und Allgemeine Lautgesetze*, Uppsala: Almquist and Wiksell, 1943.

JAKOBSON, R. (1949), 'Principes de phonologie historique', Appendix in *Principes de Phonologie* by N.S. Troubetzkoy, Paris: Editions Klincksieck. English translation by A. Keiler in KEILER (1972).

JESPERSEN, O. (1922), *Language: Its Nature, Development and Origin*, London: Allen and Unwin.

JESPERSEN, O. (1942), *A Modern English Grammar*, Copenhagen: Ejaar Munksgaard.

JOOS, M. (1961), *The Five Clocks*, New York: Harcourt Brace Jovanovich.

KAY, P. and SANKOFF, G. (1974), 'A language-universals approach to pidgins and creoles', in DECAMP and HANCOCK (1974).

KEILER, A.R. (ed.) (1972), *A Reader in Historical and Comparative Linguistics*, New York: Holt, Rinehart & Winston.

KING, R.D. (1969), *Historical Linguistics and Generative Grammar*, Englewood Cliffs, N.J.: Prentice-Hall.

KING, R.D. (1969a), 'Push chains and drag chains', *Glossa*, 3, 3–21.

KIPARSKY, P. (1968), 'Linguistic universals and linguistic change', in BACH and HARMS (1968). Also in KEILER (1972).

KIPARSKY, P. (1972), 'From paleogrammarians to neogrammarians', *York Papers in Linguistics*, 2, 33–43.

KLIMA, E. and BELLUGI, U. (1966), 'Syntactic regularities in the speech of children', in *Psycholinguistics Papers*, J. Lyons and R.J. Wales (eds), Edinburgh: Edinburgh University Press.

KOCH, M. (1974), 'A demystification of syntactic drift', *Montreal Working Papers in Linguistics*, 3, 63–114.

KRISHNAMURTI, B. (1978). 'Areal and lexical diffusion of sound change: evidence from Dravidian', *Language*, 54, 1–20.

KUNO, S. (1974), 'The position of relative clauses and conjunctions', *Linguistic Inquiry*, 5, 117–136.

LABOV, W. (1972), *Sociolinguistic Patterns*, Philadelphia: University of Pennsylvania Press.

LABOV, W. (1972a), 'Where do grammars stop?', in *Sociolinguistics: Current Trends and Prospects*, R.W. Shuy (ed.), 23rd Annual Round Table Meeting, Georgetown

254   Select Bibliography

University School of Languages and Linguistics, Georgetown: University of Georgetown Press.

LAKOFF, R. (1975), *Language and Woman's Place*, New York: Harper & Row.

LASS, R. (1976), *English Phonology and Phonological Theory: Synchronic and Diachronic Studies*, Cambridge: University Press.

LASS, R. (1980), *On Explaining Language Change*, Cambridge: University Press.

LEHMANN, W.P. (ed.) (1967), *A Reader in Nineteenth-century Historical Linguistics*, Bloomington: Indiana University Press.

LEHMANN, W.P. (1973), 'A structural principle of language and its implications', *Language*, 49, 47–66.

LENNEBERG, E.H. (1967), *Biological Foundations of Language*, New York: Wiley.

LESTER, L. and SKOUSEN, R. (1974), 'The phonology of drunkenness', *Papers from the Parasession on Natural Phonology*, Chicago: Chicago Linguistic Society.

LI, C.N. and THOMPSON, S.A. (1974), 'Historical change of word order: a case study of Chinese and its implications', in ANDERSON and JONES (1974).

LI, C.N. and THOMPSON, S.A. (1976), 'Strategies for signaling grammatical relations in Wappo', *Papers from the Twelfth Regional Meeting*, Chicago: Chicago Linguistic Society.

LIGHTFOOT, D.W. (1979), *Principles of Diachronic Syntax*, Cambridge: University Press.

LOWTH, Robert (1762) *A Short Introduction to English Grammar*, Facsimile reprint, Menston, England: The Scholar Press, 1967.

LYONS, J. (1981), *Language and Linguistics*, Cambridge: University Press.

MARTINET, A. (1955), *Economie des changements phonétiques*, Berne: A. Francke.

MARTINET, A. (1960), *Eléments de linguistique générale*, Paris: Armand Colin. English translation by E. Palmer, *Elements of General Linguistics*, London: Faber and Faber, 1964.

MEIJER, G. and MUYSKEN, P. (1977), 'On the beginnings of pidgin and creole studies: Schuchardt and Hesseling', in VALDMAN (1977).

MIHALIC, F. (1971), *The Jacaranda Dictionary and Grammar of Melanesian Pidgin*, Brisbane: Jacaranda Press.

MILROY, L (1980), *Language and Social Networks*, London: Edward Arnold.

MILROY, J. and MILROY, L. (1978), 'Belfast: change and variation in an urban vernacular' in TRUDGILL (1978).

MÜHLHÄUSLER, P. (1978), 'Samoan plantation pidgin English and the origin of New Guinea Pidgin', *Papers in Pidgin and Creole Linguistics*, I. 67–119.

MÜHLHÄUSLER, P. (1979), *Growth and structure of the lexicon of New Guinea Pidgin*, Canberra: Pacific Linguistics, C-52.

MÜHLHÄUSLER, P. (1979a), 'Sociolects in New Guinea Pidgin', in WURM (1979).

NARO, A.J. (1978) 'A study on the origins of pidginization', *Language* 54, 314–347.

O'CONNOR, J.D. (1973), *Phonetics*, Harmondsworth: Penguin.

OHALA, J.J (1974), 'Phonetic explanation in phonology', *Papers from the Parasession on Natural Phonology*, Chicago: Chicago Linguistic Society

OHALA, J.J. (1974a), 'Experimental historical phonology', in ANDERSON and JONES (1974).

OSTHOFF, C.H. and BRUGMANN, K. (1878), Preface to *Morphologische Untersuchungen auf dem Gebiete der Indogermanischen Sprachen*, I. Translated in LEHMANN (1967).

PAYNE, R. (1979), 'Humpbacks: their mysterious songs', *National Geographic* 155, 1, Jan. 1979, 18–25.

POSTAL, P.M. (1968), *Aspects of Phonological Theory*, New York: Harper & Row.

POTTER, S. (1969), *Changing English*, London: Andre Deutsch.

PROKOSCH, E. (1938), *A Comparative Germanic Grammar*, Baltimore: Linguistic Society of America.

PULLUM, G.K. (1977), 'Word order universals and grammatical relations', in *Syntax and Semantics 8: Grammatical Relations*, P. Cole and J. Sadock (eds), New York: Academic Press.

PYLES, T. (1971), *The Origins and Development of the English Language*, New York: Harcourt Brace Jovanovich.

SAFIRE, W. (1980), *On Language*, New York: Times Books.

SANKOFF, G. (1977), 'Creolization and syntactic change in New Guinea Tok Pisin', in *Sociocultural Dimensions of Language Change*, B. Blount and M. Sanches (eds), New York: Academic Press.

SANKOFF, G. and LABERGE, S. (1974), 'On the acquisition of native speakers by a language', in DECAMP and HANCOCK (1974).

SAPIR, E. (1921), *Language*, New York: Harcourt Brace.

SAUSSURE, F. de, (1915/1959), *Cours de linguistique generale*, Paris: Payot 1915. English translation by W. Baskin, *Course in General Linguistics*, New York: The Philosophical Library, 1959; London: Fontana, 1974.

SHANKWEILER, D. and HARRIS, K.S. (1966), 'An experimental approach to the problem of articulation in aphasia', *Cortex*, 2, 277–292. Also in GOODGLASS and BLUMSTEIN (1973).

SLOBIN, D.I. (1977), 'Language change in childhood and history', in *Language Learning and Thought*, J. Macnamara (ed.), New York: Academic Press, 1977.

SMITH, N.V. (1973), *The Acquisition of Phonology*, Cambridge: University Press.

SMITH, N. and WILSON, D. (1979), *Modern Linguistics. The results of Chomsky's revolution*. Harmondsworth: Penguin.

STAMPE, D. (1969), 'On the acquisition of phonetic representation', *Papers from the Fifth Regional Meeting*, Chicago: Chicago Linguistic Society.

STAMPE, D. (1979), *A Dissertation on Natural Phonology*, New York: Garland.

STURTEVANT, E.H. (1917/1961), *Linguistic Change*, Chicago: University Press, Phoenix Books edn, 1961.

TODD, L. (1974), *Pidgins and Creoles*, London: Routledge & Kegan Paul.

TRUDGILL, P. (1972), 'Sex, covert prestige and linguistic change in the urban British English of Norwich', *Language in Society*, I, 179–95.

TRUDGILL, P. (1974), *The Social Differentiation of English in Norwich*, Cambridge: Cambridge University Press.

TRUDGILL, P. (1978), *Sociolinguistic Patterns in British English*, London: Edward Arnold.

TWADDELL, W.F. (1935), 'On defining the phoneme', reprinted in *Readings in Linguistics*, M. Joos (ed.), Chicago: University Press, 1958.

VALDMAN, A. (ed.) (1977), *Pidgin and Creole Linguistics*, Bloomington: Indiana University Press.

VENDRYES, J. (1925), *Language*, London: Kegan Paul. Original title *Le Langage*, Paris: Albin Michel, 1923.

VINCENT, N. (1976), 'Perceptual factors and word order change in Latin', in HARRIS (1976).

WANG, W. (1969), 'Competing changes as a cause of residue', *Language*, 45, 9–25.

WILKINSON, A. (1967), *In Your Own Words*, London: BBC Publications.

WURM, S.A. (1979), *New Guinea and Neighboring Areas: A Sociolinguistic Laboratory*, The Hague: Mouton.

WURM, S.A., MÜHLHÄUSLER, P. and LAYCOCK, D.C. (1977), 'Language planning and engineering in Papua New Guinea', in *New Guinea Area Languages and Language Study*, vol. 3, S.A. Wurm (ed.), Canberra: Pacific Linguistics, C-40.

Acknowledgments

For kind permission to quote from copyright material the author is grateful to the following: Granada Publishing, for 'ygUDuh' by e.e. cummings, from *Complete Poems (1936–1962)*; ATV Music, 'Getting Better' © 1969 words and music by John Lennon Paul McCartney; The Bodley Head, *Zen and the Art of Motorcycle Maintenance* by Robert Pirsig; Jonathan Cape, *Bad Blood* by Richard Neville and Julia Clarke; Chatto and Windus, *Happy All the Time* by Laurie Colwin, and *The Nice and the Good* by Iris Murdoch; William Collins, *The Phantom Tollbooth* by Norton Juster; Tom Lehrer, 'When you are old and grey' © 1953 Tom Lehrer; 'Down with Mahd Drizzaws' by Spike Hughes, *Daily Telegraph Magazine*, 26 April 1968; 'Do You Say What You Really Mean?' by Anthony Lejeune, *Daily Telegraph Magazine*, 7 May 1971; review by David Holloway of *The Pocket Oxford Dictionary*, *Daily Telegraph*, 7 July 1978; Michael Joseph, *Web* by John Wyndham; J.M. Dent, 'Lament for a Dying Language' by Ogden Nash, from *Everyone but Thee and Me*, and 'Baby, what makes the sky blue?' and 'Thunder over the nursery' by Ogden Nash, from *Family Reunion*; Dennis Dobson, 'The Story of the Bald Twit Lion' by Spike Milligan, from *A Book of Milliganimals*; Faber and Faber, 'Burnt Norton' by T.S. Eliot, from *Four Quartets*; 'Who Understands What?' by Mary Stott, *Guardian*, 9 September 1968; Hamish Hamilton, *Words Fail Me* by Philip Howard; Allen Lane and the executors of the estate of Stevie Smith, 'The Jungle Husband', from *The Collected Poems of Stevie Smith* (edited by James MacGibbon); Lawrence & Wishart, *Selection from the Prison Notebooks of Antonio Gramsci* (edited by Q. Hoare and G. Nowell-Smith); Secker and Warburg, *Decadence* by Richard Gilman; Sidgwick and Jackson, *Superwoman* by Shirley Conran; Times Books Inc., *On Language* by William Safire; William Heinemann, *The Grapes of Wrath* by John Steinbeck; Grove Press Inc., *Alice's Restaurant* by Arlo Guthrie.

Index

Another Universe book by Jean Aitchison

THE ARTICULATE MAMMAL

Jean Aitchison

Is [language] a 'natural' phenomenon such as walking or sexual activity, or is it a skill which we learn, such as knitting? Why can parrots and myna birds mimic human speech although they don't understand it? Are babies born with a "blueprint" for language in their brains? In *The Articulate Mammal*, Jean Aitchison explores these and other questions that confront anyone who wants to know why we talk the way we do.

In her entertaining and informative book, the author studies slips of the tongue, speech disorders, and the language of normal adults to examine the link between what we hear and how we produce responses.

"Introduce[s] the topic of contemporary linguistics in a simple, straightforward, and intelligent manner...an excellent text." —*Choice*

"Both linguistics students and the general public should enjoy this readable introduction to psycholinguistics. Research in animal communication and theories of first-language acquisition by children are clearly presented and illustrated where necessary. The bibliography is extensive and includes the major authorities in the field. Much attention is devoted to the thinking of Noam Chomsky, though Aitchison by no means accepts all of his ideas uncritically. The book makes it quite clear that there are different schools of thought and that on many fronts, psycholinguistic research is in its infancy." —*Library Journal*

291 pp.   ISBN 0-87663-422-6

UNIVERSE INTRODUCTIONS TO LINGUISTICS
Other titles in the series

UNDERSTANDING AND PRODUCING SPEECH
Edward Matthei and Thomas Roeper

In the course of a lifetime, a human being can understand a potentially infinite number of novel sounds. How is this possible? How does the ear sort a jumble of utterances into coherent patterns? And how does the listener organize these patterns into meaningful sequences? Drawing on the latest research, Edward Matthei and Thomas Roeper examine these and other topics in their analysis of language production. They explore the seemingly effortless process of turning idea into word, word into sentence, and, conversely, someone else's sentence into ideas that we can comprehend. The action, they conclude, is actually quite complex. The authors show that understanding speech is essentially the skillful mingling of guesswork combined with a computational ability to use basic language rules.

"There's nothing like this book around anywhere—it's the sort of thing that linguists would want for their own personal libraries. I learned a lot from it, and can hardly think of a colleague of mine who would not do likewise."
—Professor Frederick J. Newmeyer, University of Washington

216 pp.

Forthcoming

LANGUAGE, MEANING AND CONTEXT by John Lyons
Outlines recent theories of linguistic semantics and assesses their strengths and weaknesses, stressing the interlocking system upon which language is based.

SYNTAX TODAY by Keith Brown
A popular, simple survey of the main lines of development in grammatical theory.

LANGUAGE AND SOCIETY by William Downes
The interaction between the various social factors involved in sociolinguistics, from geographical location and ethnic origin to social class and sex.

UNIVERSE BOOKS
381 Park Avenue South New York, N.Y. 10016